Core Data
by Tutorials

Aaron Douglas, Matthew Morey and Pietro Rea

Core Data by Tutorials

Aaron Douglas, Matthew Morey and Pietro Rea

Copyright ©2019 Razeware LLC.

ISBN: 978-1-950325-04-7

Dedications

"To my husband, Mike, who puts up with all my weird quirks and supports all the things I do."

— *Aaron Douglas*

"To my amazing wife Tricia and my parents — Thanks for always supporting me."

— *Matthew Morey*

"To my wonderful wife Emily, my daughter Rose, and my parents. Thank you for always supporting me every step of the way."

— *Pietro Rea*

About the Authors

Aaron Douglas was that kid taking apart the mechanical and electrical appliances at five years of age to see how they worked. He never grew out of that core interest - to know how things work. He took an early interest in computer programming, figuring out how to get past security to be able to play games on his dad's computer. He's still that feisty nerd, but at least now he gets paid to do it. Aaron works for Automattic ((WordPress.com, WooCommerce, Tumblr, Simplenote) as a Mobile Lead primarily on the WooCommerce mobile apps. Find Aaron on Twitter as @astralbodies and on his blog at https://aaron.blog.

Matthew Morey is an engineer, developer, hacker, creator, and tinkerer. As an active member of the mobile community and head of technology at Valtech he has led numerous successful mobile projects worldwide. He's the creator of Buoy Explorer, a marine conditions app for water sports enthusiast, and Wrist Presenter, an app that lets you control presentations wirelessly with your smart watch. When not developing apps he enjoys traveling, snowboarding, and surfing. He blogs about technology and business at matthewmorey.com.

Pietro Rea is a senior software engineer at Upside Travel in Washington D.C. Pietro's work has been featured in the App Store across several categories: media, e-commerce, lifestyle and more. Having worked at Fortune 500 companies and venture-backed startups, Pietro has a passion for building apps users can't live without. You can find Pietro on Twitter as @pietrorea.

About the Editors

Darren Ferguson is the technical editor for this book. He is an experienced software developer and works for M.C. Dean, Inc, a systems integration provider from North Virginia. When he's not coding, you'll find him enjoying EPL Football, traveling as much as possible and spending time with his wife and daughter. Find Darren on Twitter as @darren102.

Rich Turton is the final pass editor of this book. Rich is an iOS developer for MartianCraft and long-time contributor to raywenderlich.com. When he's not in front of a computer he is usually trying to play the piano, trying to make fancy cocktails, or trying to play elaborate Lego games with his daughters. Sometimes all at the same time.

About the Artist

Vicki Wenderlich is the designer and artist of the cover of this book. She is Ray's wife and business partner. She is a digital artist who creates illustrations, game art and a lot of other art or design work for the tutorials and books on raywenderlich.com. When she's not making art, she loves hiking, a good glass of wine and attempting to create the perfect cheese plate.

Table of Contents

Introduction

What is Core Data? You'll hear a variety of answers to this question: It's a database! It's SQLite! It's not a database! And so forth.

Here's the technical answer: Core Data is an object graph management and persistence framework in the macOS and iOS SDKs.

That means Core Data can store and retrieve data, but it isn't a relational database like MySQL or SQLite. Although it can use SQLite as the data store behind the scenes, you don't think about Core Data in terms of tables and rows and primary keys.

Imagine you're writing an app to keep track of dining habits. You have a varied set of objects: restaurant objects, each with properties such as name and address; categories, to organize the restaurants; and visits, to log each visit to a restaurant.

The object graph in memory might look something like this:

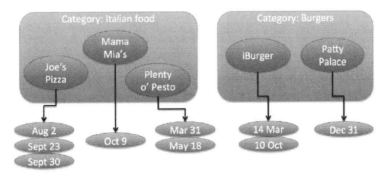

Object graph management means Core Data works with objects that you define, such as the ones in the diagram above. For example, each restaurant (represented by a red bubble) would have a property pointing back to the category object. It would also have a property holding the list of visits.

Since UIKit is an object-oriented framework, you're probably storing data in objects already. Core Data builds on this to keep track of the objects and their relationships to each other. You can imagine expanding the graph to include what the user ordered, ratings and so on.

Persistence means the data is stored somewhere durable such as the device's flash memory or "the cloud." You point to the entire graph and just say "save."

When your app launches, you just say "load" and the entire object graph pops up in memory again, ready for use. That's Core Data at work!

Maybe your users eat out a lot and have thousands of restaurant visits — rest assured Core Data is smart about lazily loading objects and caching to optimize both memory usage and speed. Core Data has many other features aside from simply storing and fetching data:

You can perform custom filtering with predicates, sort the data and and calculate statistics. You'll learn all about these features and more in this book.

We've updated all the chapters in this book for Swift 5.1, iOS 13 and Xcode 11.

Who this book is for

This book is for iOS developers who already know the basics of iOS and Swift, and want to learn Core Data.

If you're a complete beginner to iOS, we suggest you read through The iOS Apprentice first. That will give you a solid foundation in building iOS apps from the ground-up.

If you know the basics of iOS development but are new to Swift, we suggest you read Swift Apprentice first. That book has a similar hands-on approach and takes you on a comprehensive tour through the Swift language.

You can find both of these prerequisite books at our store: http://store.raywenderlich.com

How to use this book

This book will teach you the fundamentals of Core Data by means of hands-on tutorials. You'll jump right into building a Core Data app in Chapter 1, as we think most people learn best by doing. We encourage you to type along with the instructions in the book.

If you're new to Core Data or want to review the basics, we suggest you start with Chapters 1–3. These chapters cover the fundamentals of Core Data and you'll need the knowledge in them to understand the rest of the book.

Otherwise, we suggest a pragmatic approach. Each chapter stands on its own, so you can pick and choose the chapters that interest you the most.

What's in store

Here's a quick summary of what you'll find in each chapter:

1. Chapter 1, Your First Core Data App: You'll click File\New Project and write a Core Data app from scratch! This chapter covers the basics of setting up your data model and then adding and fetching records.

2. Chapter 2, NSManagedObject Subclasses: NSManagedObject is the base data storage class of your Core Data object graphs. This chapter will teach you how you customize your own managed object subclasses to store and validate data.

3. Chapter 3, The Core Data Stack: Under the hood, Core Data is made up of many parts working together. In this chapter, you'll learn about how these parts fit together, and move away from the starter Xcode template to build your own customizable system.

4. Chapter 4, Intermediate Fetching: Your apps will fetch data all the time, and Core Data offers many options for getting the data to you efficiently. This chapter covers more advanced fetch requests, predicates, sorting and asynchronous fetching.

5. Chapter 5, NSFetchedResultsController: Table views are at the core of many iOS apps, and Apple wants to make Core Data play nicely with them! In this chapter, you'll learn how NSFetchedResultsController can save you time and code when your table views are backed by data from Core Data.

6. Chapter 6, Versioning and Migration: As you update and enhance your app, its data model will almost certainly need to change. In this chapter, you'll learn how to create multiple versions of your data model and then migrate your users forward so they can keep their existing data as they upgrade.

7. Chapter 7, Unit Tests: Testing is an important part of the development process, and you shouldn't leave Core Data out of that! In this chapter, you'll learn how to set up a separate test environment for Core Data and see examples of how to test your models.

8. Chapter 8, Measuring and Boosting Performance: No one ever complained that an app was too fast, so it's important to be vigilant about tracking performance. In this chapter, you'll learn how to measure your app's performance with various Xcode tools and then pick up some tips for dealing with slow spots in your code.

9. Chapter 9, Multiple Managed Object Contexts: In this chapter, you'll expand the usual Core Data stack to include multiple managed object contexts. You'll learn how this can improve perceived performance and help make your app architecture less monolithic and more compartmentalized.

What You Need

To follow along with the tutorials in this book, you'll need the following:

- A Mac running macOS Catalina or later. You'll need this to be able to install the latest version of Xcode.

- Xcode 11.0 or later. Xcode is the main development tool for iOS. You can download the latest version of Xcode from Apple's developer site here: apple.co/2asi58y

You can use the iOS 13 Simulator that comes with Xcode for all of the chapters.

Once you have these items in place, you'll be able to follow along with every chapter in this book.

Book Source Code & Forums

If you bought the digital edition

The digital edition of this book comes with the source code for the starter and completed projects for each chapter. These resources are included with the digital edition you downloaded from store.raywenderlich.com.

The digital edition of this book also comes with free access to any future updates we may make to the book!

The best way to get update notifications is to sign up for our monthly newsletter. This includes a list of the tutorials that came out on raywenderlich.com that month, any important news like book updates or new books, and a list of our favorite iOS development links for that month. You can sign up here:

- www.raywenderlich.com/newsletter

If you bought the print version

You can get the source code for the print edition of the book here:

https://store.raywenderlich.com/products/core-data-by-tutorials-source-code

Forums

We've also set up an official forum for the book at forums.raywenderlich.com. This is a great place to ask questions about the book or to submit any errors you may find.

Digital book editions

We have a digital edition of this book available in both ePUB and PDF, which can be handy if you want a soft copy to take with you, or you want to quickly search for a specific term within the book.

Buying the digital edition version of the book also has a few extra benefits: free updates each time we update the book, access to older versions of the book, and you can download the digital editions from anywhere, at anytime.

Visit our book store page here:

- https://store.raywenderlich.com/products/core-data-by-tutorials.

And if you purchased the print version of this book, you're eligible to upgrade to the digital editions at a significant discount! Simply email support@razeware.com with your receipt for the physical copy and we'll get you set up with the discounted digital edition version of the book.

Book License

By purchasing *Core Data by Tutorials*, you have the following license:

- You are allowed to use and/or modify the source code in *Core Data by Tutorials* in as many apps as you want, with no attribution required.

- You are allowed to use and/or modify all art, images and designs that are included in *Core Data by Tutorials* in as many apps as you want, but must include this attribution line somewhere inside your app: "Artwork/images/designs: from *Core Data by Tutorials* book, available at http://www.raywenderlich.com."

- The source code included in *Core Data by Tutorials* is for your personal use only. You are NOT allowed to distribute or sell the source code in *Core Data by Tutorials* without prior authorization.

- This book is for your personal use only. You are NOT allowed to sell this book without prior authorization or distribute it to friends, co-workers or students; they would need to purchase their own copies.

Chapter 1: Your First Core Data App

By Pietro Rea

Welcome to Core Data!

In this chapter, you'll write your very first Core Data app. You'll see how easy it is to get started with all the resources provided in Xcode, from starter code templates to the Data Model editor.

You're going to hit the ground running right from the start. By the end of the chapter you'll know how to:

- Model data using Xcode's model editor

- Add new records to Core Data

- Fetch a set of records from Core Data

- Display the fetched records using a table view.

You'll also get a sense of what Core Data is doing behind the scenes, and how you can interact with the various moving pieces. This will put you well on your way to understanding the next two chapters, which continue the introduction to Core Data with more advanced models and data validation.

Getting started

Open Xcode and create a new iOS project based on the **Single View App** template. Name the app **HitList** and make sure **Use Core Data** is checked.

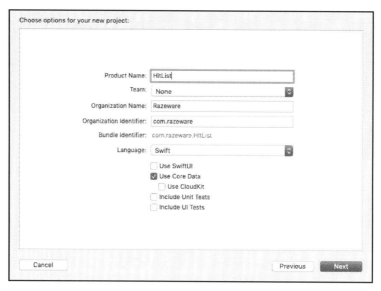

Checking the **Use Core Data** box will cause Xcode to generate boilerplate code for what's known as an NSPersistentContainer in **AppDelegate.swift**.

The NSPersistentContainer consists of a set of objects that facilitate saving and retrieving information from Core Data. Inside this container is an object to manage the Core Data state as a whole, an object representing the Data Model, and so on.

You'll learn about each of these pieces in the first few chapters. Later, you'll even have the chance to write your own Core Data stack! The standard stack works well for most apps, but depending on your your app and its data requirements, you can customize the stack to be more efficient.

> **Note:** Not all Xcode templates under iOS ▸ Application have the option to start with Core Data. In Xcode 11, only the **Master-Detail App**, the **Tabbed App** and the **Single View App** templates have the **Use Core Data** checkbox.

The idea for this sample app is simple: There will be a table view with a list of names for your very own "hit list". You'll be able to add names to this list, and eventually, use Core Data to make sure the data is stored between sessions.

We don't condone violence in this book, so you can think of this app as a favorites list to keep track of your friends too, of course!

Click on **Main.storyboard** to open it in Interface Builder. Select the view controller on the canvas and embed it inside a navigation controller. From Xcode's **Editor** menu, select **Embed In...** ▸ **Navigation Controller**.

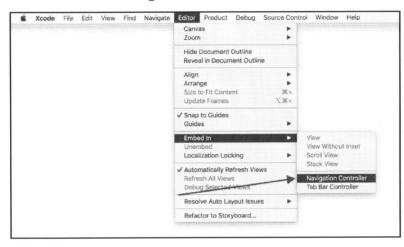

Next, drag a **Table View** from the object library into the view controller, then resize it so it covers the entire view.

If not already open, use the icon located in the lower left corner of your canvas to open Interface Builder's document outline.

Ctrl-drag from the **Table View** in the document outline to its parent view and select the **Leading Space to Safe Area** constraint:

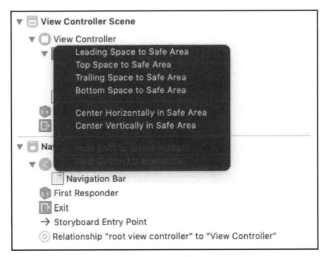

Do this three more times, selecting the constraints **Trailing Space to Safe Area**, **Top Space to Safe Area** and finally, **Bottom Space to Safe Area**. Adding those four constraints will make the table view fill its parent view.

Next, drag a **Bar Button Item** and place it on the view controller's navigation bar. Finally, select the bar button item and change its system item to **Add**.

Your canvas should look similar to the following screenshot:

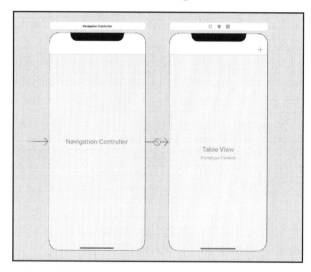

Every time you tap the **Add** button, an alert controller containing a text field will appear. From there, you'll be able to type someone's name into the text field. Tapping Save will save the name, dismiss the alert controller and refresh the table view, displaying all the names you've entered.

But first, you need to make the view controller the table view's data source. In the canvas, Ctrl-drag from the table view to the yellow view controller icon above the navigation bar, as shown below, and click on **dataSource**:

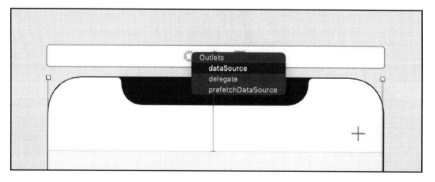

In case you're wondering, you don't need to set up the table view's delegate since tapping on the cells won't trigger any action. It doesn't get simpler than this!

Open the assistant editor by pressing Control-Command-Option-Enter or by selecting the adjust editors button in the top right of the Storyboard scene and choosing Assistant as shown below.

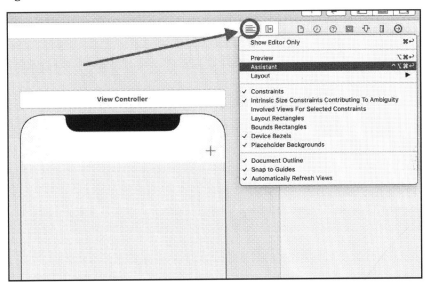

Ctrl-drag from the table view onto **ViewController.swift** inside the class definition to create an IBOutlet.

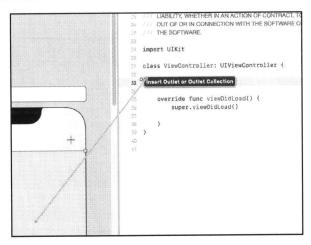

Next, name the new IBOutlet property tableView, resulting in the following line:

```
@IBOutlet weak var tableView: UITableView!
```

Next, Ctrl-drag from the **Add** button into **ViewController.swift** just below your `viewDidLoad()` definition. This time, create an action instead of an outlet, naming the method `addName`, with a type `UIBarButtonItem`:

```
@IBAction func addName(_ sender: UIBarButtonItem) {

}
```

You can now refer to the table view and the bar button item's action in code.

Next, you'll set up the model for the table view. Add the following property to **ViewController.swift** below the `tableView IBOutlet`:

```
var names: [String] = []
```

`names` is a mutable array holding string values displayed by the table view. Next, replace the implementation of `viewDidLoad()` with the following:

```
override func viewDidLoad() {
  super.viewDidLoad()

  title = "The List"
  tableView.register(UITableViewCell.self,
                 forCellReuseIdentifier: "Cell")
}
```

This will set a title on the navigation bar and register the `UITableViewCell` class with the table view.

> **Note**: `register(_:forCellReuseIdentifier:)` guarantees your table view will return a cell of the correct type when the **Cell** `reuseIdentifier` is provided to the dequeue method.

Next, still in **ViewController.swift**, add the following `UITableViewDataSource` extension below your class definition for `ViewController`:

```
// MARK: - UITableViewDataSource
extension ViewController: UITableViewDataSource {

  func tableView(_ tableView: UITableView,
              numberOfRowsInSection section: Int) -> Int {
    return names.count
  }

  func tableView(_ tableView: UITableView,
```

```
                        cellForRowAt indexPath: IndexPath)
                    -> UITableViewCell {

    let cell =
      tableView.dequeueReusableCell(withIdentifier: "Cell",
                                    for: indexPath)
    cell.textLabel?.text = names[indexPath.row]
    return cell
  }
}
```

If you've ever worked with UITableView, this code should look very familiar. First you return the number of rows in the table as the number of items in your names array.

Next, tableView(_:cellForRowAt:) dequeues table view cells and populates them with the corresponding string from the names array.

Next, you need a way to add new names so the table view can display them. Implement the addName IBAction method you Ctrl-dragged into your code earlier:

```
// Implement the addName IBAction
@IBAction func addName(_ sender: UIBarButtonItem) {

  let alert = UIAlertController(title: "New Name",
                               message: "Add a new name",
                               preferredStyle: .alert)

  let saveAction = UIAlertAction(title: "Save",
                                 style: .default) {
    [unowned self] action in

    guard let textField = alert.textFields?.first,
      let nameToSave = textField.text else {
        return
    }

    self.names.append(nameToSave)
    self.tableView.reloadData()
  }

  let cancelAction = UIAlertAction(title: "Cancel",
                                   style: .cancel)

  alert.addTextField()

  alert.addAction(saveAction)
  alert.addAction(cancelAction)

  present(alert, animated: true)
}
```

Every time you tap the **Add** button, this method will present a `UIAlertController` with a text field and two buttons: **Save** and **Cancel**.

Save inserts the text fields current text into the `names` array then reloads the table view. Since the `names` array is the model backing the table view, whatever you type into the text field will appear in the table view.

Finally, build and run your app for the first time. Next, tap the **Add** button. The alert controller will look like this:

Add four or five names to the list. You should see something similar to below:

Your table view will display the data and your array will store the names, but the big thing missing here is **persistence**. The array is in memory but if you force quit the app or reboot your device, your hit list will be wiped out. Core Data provides persistence, meaning it can store data in a more durable state so it can outlive an app re-launch or a device reboot.

You haven't added any Core Data elements yet, so nothing should persist after you navigate away from the app. Let's test this out. Press the Home button if you're using a physical device or the equivalent (Shift + ⌘ + H) if you're using the Simulator. This will take you back to the familiar app grid on the home screen:

From the home screen, tap the **HitList** icon to bring the app back to the foreground. The names are still on the screen. What happened?

When you tap the Home button, the app currently in the foreground goes to the background. When this happens, the operating system flash-freezes everything currently in memory, including the strings in the names array. Similarly, when it's time to wake up and return to the foreground, the operating system restores what used to be in memory as if you'd never left.

Apple introduced these advances in multitasking back in iOS 4. They create a seamless experience for iOS users but add a wrinkle to the definition of persistence for iOS developers. Are the names really persisted?

No, not really. If you had completely killed the app in the fast app switcher or turned off your phone, those names would be gone. You can verify this as well. With the app in the foreground, enter the fast app switcher.

You can do this by either double tapping the Home button if your device has one or slowly dragging upwards from the bottom of the screen if you're on an iPhone X or later.

From here, flick the HitList app snapshot upwards to terminate the app. After you remove the app from the app switcher, there should be no trace of HitList in living memory (no pun intended). Verify the names are gone by returning to the home screen and tapping on the HitList icon to trigger a fresh launch.

The difference between flash-freezing and persistence may be obvious if you've worked with iOS for some time and are familiar with the way multitasking works. In a user's mind, however, there is no difference. The user doesn't care *why* the names are still there, whether the app went into the background and came back, or because the app saved and reloaded them. All that matters is the names are still there when the app comes back!

So the real test of persistence is whether your data is still there after a fresh app launch.

Modeling your data

Now you know how to check for persistence, you can dive into Core Data. Your goal for the HitList app is simple: persist the names you enter so they're available for viewing after a fresh app launch.

Up to this point, you've been using plain old Swift strings to store the names in memory. In this section, you'll replace these strings with Core Data objects. The first step is to create a **managed object model**, which describes the way Core Data represents data on disk.

By default, Core Data uses a SQLite database as the persistent store, so you can think of the Data Model as the database schema.

> **Note**: You'll come across the word *managed* quite a bit in this book. If you see "managed" in the name of a class, such as in `NSManagedObjectContext`, chances are you are dealing with a Core Data class. "Managed" refers to Core Data's management of the life cycle of Core Data objects.
>
> However, don't assume all Core Data classes contain the word "managed". Most don't. For a comprehensive list of Core Data classes, check out the Core Data framework reference in the documentation browser.

Since you've elected to use Core Data, Xcode automatically created a Data Model file for you and named it **HitList.xcdatamodeld**.

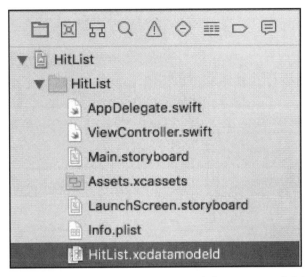

Open **HitList.xcdatamodeld**. As you can see, Xcode has a powerful Data Model editor:

The Data Model editor has a lot of features you'll explore in later chapters. For now, let's focus on creating a single Core Data entity.

Click on **Add Entity** on the lower-left to create a new entity. Double-click the new entity and change its name to **Person**, like so:

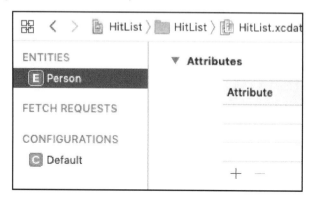

You may be wondering why the model editor uses the term Entity. Weren't you simply defining a new class? As you'll see shortly, Core Data comes with its own vocabulary. Here's a quick rundown of some terms you'll commonly encounter:

- An **entity** is a class definition in Core Data. The classic example is an Employee or a Company. In a relational database, an entity corresponds to a table.

- An **attribute** is a piece of information attached to a particular entity. For example, an Employee entity could have attributes for the employee's name, position and salary. In a database, an attribute corresponds to a particular field in a table.

- A **relationship** is a link between multiple entities. In Core Data, relationships between two entities are called **to-one relationships**, while those between one and many entities are called **to-many relationships**. For example, a Manager can have a **to-many relationship** with a set of employees, whereas an individual Employee will usually have a **to-one relationship** with his manager.

> **Note**: You've probably noticed entities sound a lot like classes. Likewise, attributes and relationships sound a lot like properties. What's the difference? You can think of a Core Data entity as a class definition and the managed object as an instance of that class.

Now you know what an attribute is, you can add an attribute to Person object created earlier. Still in **HitList.xcdatamodeld**, select Person on the left-hand side and click the plus sign (+) under **Attributes**.

Set the new attribute's name to, er, **name** and change its type to **String**:

In Core Data, an attribute can be of one of several data types. You'll learn about these in the next few chapters.

Saving to Core Data

Open **ViewController.swift**, add the following Core Data module import below the UIKit import:

```
import CoreData
```

This import is all you need to start using the Core Data API in your code.

Next, replace the names property definition with the following:

```
var people: [NSManagedObject] = []
```

You'll store Person entities rather than string names, so you rename the array serving as the table view's data model to people. It now holds instances of NSManagedObject rather than simple strings.

NSManagedObject represents a single object stored in Core Data; you must use it to create, edit, save and delete from your Core Data persistent store. As you'll see shortly, NSManagedObject is a shape-shifter. It can take the form of any entity in your Data Model, appropriating whatever attributes and relationships you defined.

Since you're changing the table view's model, you must also replace both data source methods implemented earlier. Replace your `UITableViewDataSource` extension with the following:

```
// MARK: - UITableViewDataSource
extension ViewController: UITableViewDataSource {
  func tableView(_ tableView: UITableView,
                 numberOfRowsInSection section: Int) -> Int {
    return people.count
  }

  func tableView(_ tableView: UITableView,
                 cellForRowAt indexPath: IndexPath)
                 -> UITableViewCell {

    let person = people[indexPath.row]
    let cell =
      tableView.dequeueReusableCell(withIdentifier: "Cell",
                                    for: indexPath)
    cell.textLabel?.text =
      person.value(forKeyPath: "name") as? String
    return cell
  }
}
```

The most significant change to these methods occurs in `tableView(_:cellForRowAt:)`. Instead of matching cells with the corresponding string in the model array, you now match cells with the corresponding `NSManagedObject`. Note how you grab the name attribute from the `NSManagedObject`. It happens here:

```
cell.textLabel?.text =
  person.value(forKeyPath: "name") as? String
```

Why do you have to do this? As it turns out, `NSManagedObject` doesn't know about the name attribute you defined in your Data Model, so there's no way of accessing it directly with a property. The only way Core Data provides to read the value is **key-value coding**, commonly referred to as KVC.

Note: KVC is a mechanism in Foundation for accessing an object's properties indirectly using strings. In this case, KVC makes `NSManagedObject` behave somewhat like a dictionary at runtime.

Key-value coding is available to all classes inheriting from `NSObject`, including `NSManagedObject`. You can't access properties using KVC on a Swift object that doesn't descend from `NSObject`.

Next, find addName(_:) and replace the save UIAlertAction with the following:

```
let saveAction = UIAlertAction(title: "Save", style: .default) {
  [unowned self] action in

  guard let textField = alert.textFields?.first,
    let nameToSave = textField.text else {
      return
  }

  self.save(name: nameToSave)
  self.tableView.reloadData()
}
```

This takes the text in the text field and passes it over to a new method named save(name:). Xcode complains because save(name:) doesn't exist yet. Add it below addName(_:):

```
func save(name: String) {

  guard let appDelegate =
    UIApplication.shared.delegate as? AppDelegate else {
    return
  }

  // 1
  let managedContext =
    appDelegate.persistentContainer.viewContext

  // 2
  let entity =
    NSEntityDescription.entity(forEntityName: "Person",
                               in: managedContext)!

  let person = NSManagedObject(entity: entity,
                               insertInto: managedContext)

  // 3
  person.setValue(name, forKeyPath: "name")

  // 4
  do {
    try managedContext.save()
    people.append(person)
  } catch let error as NSError {
    print("Could not save. \(error), \(error.userInfo)")
  }
}
```

This is where Core Data kicks in! Here's what the code does:

1. Before you can save or retrieve anything from your Core Data store, you first need to get your hands on an `NSManagedObjectContext`. You can consider a managed object context as an in-memory "scratchpad" for working with managed objects.

   Think of saving a new managed object to Core Data as a two-step process: first, you insert a new managed object into a managed object context; once you're happy, you "commit" the changes in your managed object context to save it to disk.

   Xcode has already generated a managed object context as part of the new project's template. Remember, this only happens if you check the **Use Core Data** checkbox at the beginning. This default managed object context lives as a property of the `NSPersistentContainer` in the application delegate. To access it, you first get a reference to the app delegate.

2. You create a new managed object and insert it into the managed object context. You can do this in one step with `NSManagedObject`'s static method: `entity(forEntityName:in:)`.

   You may be wondering what an `NSEntityDescription` is all about. Recall earlier, `NSManagedObject` was called a shape-shifter class because it can represent any entity. An entity description is the piece linking the entity definition from your Data Model with an instance of `NSManagedObject` at runtime.

3. With an `NSManagedObject` in hand, you set the `name` attribute using key-value coding. You must spell the KVC key (name in this case) **exactly** as it appears in your Data Model, otherwise, your app will crash at runtime.

4. You commit your changes to `person` and save to disk by calling `save` on the managed object context. Note `save` can throw an error, which is why you call it using the `try` keyword within a `do-catch` block. Finally, insert the new managed object into the `people` array so it shows up when the table view reloads.

That's a little more complicated than using an array of strings, but not too bad. Some of the code here, such as getting the managed object context and entity, could be done just once in your own `init()` or `viewDidLoad()` then reused later. For simplicity, you're doing it all in the same method.

Build and run the app, and add a few names to the table view:

If the names are actually stored in Core Data, the HitList app should pass the persistence test. With the app in the foreground, go to the fast app switcher and then terminate it.

From Springboard, tap the HitList app to trigger a fresh launch. Wait, what happened? The table view is empty:

You saved to Core Data, but after a fresh app launch, the people array is empty! That's because the data is sitting on disk waiting for you, but you're not showing it yet.

Fetching from Core Data

To get data from your persistent store into the managed object context, you have to **fetch** it. Open **ViewController.swift** and add the following below `viewDidLoad()`:

```swift
override func viewWillAppear(_ animated: Bool) {
  super.viewWillAppear(animated)

  //1
  guard let appDelegate =
    UIApplication.shared.delegate as? AppDelegate else {
      return
  }

  let managedContext =
    appDelegate.persistentContainer.viewContext

  //2
  let fetchRequest =
    NSFetchRequest<NSManagedObject>(entityName: "Person")

  //3
  do {
    people = try managedContext.fetch(fetchRequest)
  } catch let error as NSError {
    print("Could not fetch. \(error), \(error.userInfo)")
  }
}
```

Step by step, this is what the code does:

1. Before you can do anything with Core Data, you need a managed object context. Fetching is no different! Like before, you pull up the application delegate and grab a reference to its persistent container to get your hands on its `NSManagedObjectContext`.

2. As the name suggests, `NSFetchRequest` is the class responsible for fetching from Core Data. Fetch requests are both powerful and flexible. You can use fetch requests to fetch a set of objects meeting the provided criteria (i.e. give me all employees living in Wisconsin and have been with the company at least three years), individual values (i.e., give me the longest name in the database) and more.

    Fetch requests have several qualifiers used to refine the set of results returned. You'll learn more about these qualifiers in Chapter 4, "Intermediate Fetching"; for now, you should know `NSEntityDescription` is one of these required qualifiers.

Setting a fetch request's entity property, or alternatively initializing it with init(entityName:), fetches *all* objects of a particular entity. This is what you do here to fetch all Person entities. Also note NSFetchRequest is a generic type. This use of generics specifies a fetch request's *expected* return type, in this case NSManagedObject.

3. You hand the fetch request over to the managed object context to do the heavy lifting. fetch(_:) returns an array of managed objects meeting the criteria specified by the fetch request.

> **Note**: Like save(), fetch(_:) can also throw an error so you have to use it within a do block. If an error occurred during the fetch, you can inspect the error inside the catch block and respond appropriately.

Build and run the application. Immediately, you should see the list of names you added earlier:

Great! They're back from the dead (pun intended). Add a few more names to the list and restart the app to verify saving and fetching are working. Short of deleting the app, resetting the Simulator or throwing your phone off a tall building, the names will appear in the table view no matter what.

Note: There were a few rough edges in this sample app: you had to get the managed object context from the app delegate each time, and you used KVC to access an entity's attributes rather than a more natural object-style `person.name`.

There are better ways to save and fetch data from Core Data, which you'll explore in future chapters. The purpose of doing it the "long way" here is to learn what's going on behind the scenes!

Key points

- Core Data provides **on-disk persistence**, which means your data will be accessible even after terminating your app or shutting down your device. This is different from in-memory persistence, which will only save your data as long as your app is in memory, either in the foreground or in the background.

- Xcode comes with a powerful **Data Model editor**, which you can use to create your **managed object model**.

- A managed object model is made up of **entities**, **attributes** and **relationships**

- An **entity** is a class definition in Core Data.

- An **attribute** is a piece of information attached to an entity.

- A **relationship** is a link between multiple entities.

- An `NSManagedObject` is a run-time representation of a Core Data entity. You can read and write to its attributes using **Key-Value Coding**.

- You need an `NSManagedObjectContext` to `save()` or `fetch(_:)` data to and from Core Data.

Chapter 2: NSManagedObject Subclasses

By Pietro Rea

You got your feet wet with a simple Core Data app in Chapter 1; now it's time to explore more of what Core Data has to offer!

At the core of this chapter is the subclassing of NSManagedObject to make your own classes for each data entity. This creates a direct one-to-one mapping between entities in the data model editor and classes in your code. This means in some parts of your code, you can work with objects and properties without worrying too much about the Core Data side of things.

Along the way, you'll learn about all the data types available in Core Data entities, including a few outside the usual string and number types. And with all the data type options available, you'll also learn about validating data to automatically check values before saving.

Getting started

Head over to the files accompanying this book and open the sample project named **BowTies** in the starter folder. Like **HitList**, this project uses Xcode's Core Data-enabled **Single View App** template. And like before, this means Xcode generated its own ready-to-use Core Data stack located in **AppDelegate.swift**.

Open **Main.storyboard**. Here you'll find the sample project's single-page UI:

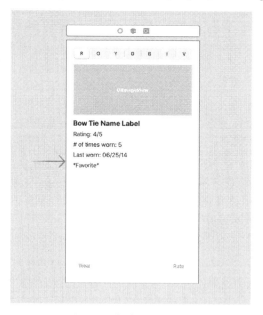

As you can probably guess, BowTies is a lightweight bow tie management application. You can switch between the different colors of bow ties you own — the app assumes one of each — using the topmost segmented control. Tap "R" for red, "O" for orange and so on.

Tapping on a particular color pulls up an image of the tie and populates several labels on the screen with specific information about the tie. This includes:

• The name of the bow tie (so you can tell similarly-colored ones apart)

• The number of times you've worn the tie

• The date you last wore the tie

• Whether the tie is a favorite of yours

The **Wear** button on the bottom-left increments the number of times you've worn that particular tie and sets the last worn date to today.

Orange is not your color? Not to worry. The **Rate** button on the bottom-right changes a bow tie's rating. This particular rating system uses a scale from 0 to 5, allowing for decimal values.

That's what the application is **supposed** to do in its final state. Open **ViewController.swift** to see what it currently does:

```swift
import UIKit

class ViewController: UIViewController {

  // MARK: - IBOutlets
  @IBOutlet weak var segmentedControl: UISegmentedControl!
  @IBOutlet weak var imageView: UIImageView!
  @IBOutlet weak var nameLabel: UILabel!
  @IBOutlet weak var ratingLabel: UILabel!
  @IBOutlet weak var timesWornLabel: UILabel!
  @IBOutlet weak var lastWornLabel: UILabel!
  @IBOutlet weak var favoriteLabel: UILabel!
  @IBOutlet weak var wearButton: UIButton!
  @IBOutlet weak var rateButton: UIButton!

  // MARK: - View Life Cycle
  override func viewDidLoad() {
    super.viewDidLoad()
  }

  // MARK: - IBActions
  @IBAction func segmentedControl(
    _ sender: UISegmentedControl) {

  }

  @IBAction func wear(_ sender: UIButton) {

  }

  @IBAction func rate(_ sender: UIButton) {

  }
}
```

The bad news is in its current state, BowTies doesn't do anything. The good news is you don't need to do any Ctrl-dragging!

The segmented control and all the labels on the user interface are already connected to IBOutlets in code. In addition, the segmented control, Wear and Rate button all have corresponding IBActions.

It looks like you have everything you need to get started adding some Core Data — but wait, what are you going to display onscreen? There's no input method to speak of, so the app must ship with sample data.That's exactly right. BowTies includes a property list called **SampleData.plist** containing the information for seven sample ties, one for each color of the rainbow.

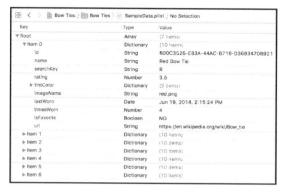

Furthermore, the application's asset catalog **Assets.xcassets** contains seven images corresponding to the seven bow ties in **SampleData.plist**.

What you have to do now is take this sample data, store it in Core Data and use it to implement the bow tie management functionality.

Modeling your data

In the previous chapter, you learned one of the first things you have to do when starting a new Core Data project is create your data model.

Open **BowTies.xcdatamodeld** and click **Add Entity** on the lower-left to create a new entity. Double-click on the new entity and change its name to **BowTie**, like so:

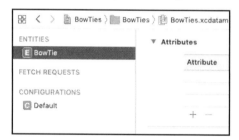

In the previous chapter, you created a simple `Person` entity with a single string attribute to hold the person's name. Core Data supports several other data types, and you'll use most of them for the new `BowTie` entity.

An attribute's data type determines what kind of data you can store in it and how much space it will occupy on disk. In Core Data, an attribute's data type begins as `Undefined` so you'll have to change it to something else.

If you remember from **SampleData.plist**, each bow tie has ten associated pieces of information. This means the `BowTie` entity will end up with at least ten attributes in the model editor.

Select `BowTie` on the left-hand side and click the plus sign (+) under **Attributes**. Change the new attribute's name to **name** and set its type to **String**:

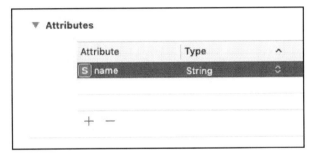

Repeat this process seven more times to add the following attributes:

- A **Boolean** named **isFavorite**

- A **Date** named **lastWorn**

- A **Double** named **rating**

- A **String** named **searchKey**

- An **Integer 32** named **timesWorn**

- A **UUID** named **id**

- A **URI** named **url**

Most of these data types are common in everyday programming. If you haven't heard of a **UUID** before, it's short for **universally unique identifier** and it's commonly used to uniquely identify information.

URI stands for **uniform resource identifier** and it's used to name and identify different resources like files and web pages. In fact, all URLs are URIs!

When you're finished, your Attributes section should look similar to the following:

Attribute	Type	
id	UUID	
lastWorn	Date	
isFavorite	Boolean	
name	String	
searchKey	String	
rating	Double	
timesWorn	Integer 32	
url	URI	

Don't worry if the order of the attributes is different — all that matters is the attribute names and types are correct.

Note: You may have noticed you have three options for the `timesWorn` integer attribute: **Integer 16**, **Integer 32** or **Integer 64**.

16, 32 and 64 refer to the number of bits representing the integer. This is important for two reasons: the number of bits reflects how much space an integer takes up on disk as well as how many values it can represent, also known as its range. Here are the ranges for the three types of integers:

Range for 16-bit integer: -32768 to 32767

Range for 32-bit integer: −2147483648 to 2147483647

Range for 64-bit integer: −9223372036854775808 to 9223372036854775807

How do you choose? The source of your data will dictate the best type of integer. You are assuming your users *really* like bow ties, so a 32-bit integer should offer enough storage for a lifetime of bow tie wear.

Each bow tie has an associated image. How will you store it in Core Data? Add one more attribute to the BowTie entity, name it **photoData** and change its data type to **Binary Data**:

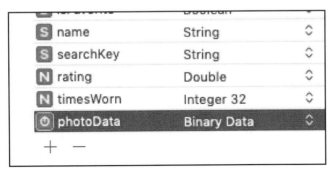

Core Data provides the option of storing arbitrary blobs of binary data directly in your data model. These could be anything from images, to PDF files, to anything that can be serialized into zeroes and ones.

As you can imagine, this convenience can come at a steep cost. Storing a large amount of binary data in the same SQLite database as your other attributes will likely impact your app's performance. That means a giant binary blob would be loaded into memory each time you access an entity, even if you only need to access its name!

Luckily, Core Data anticipates this problem. With the photoData attribute selected, open the **Attributes Inspector** and check the **Allows External Storage** option.

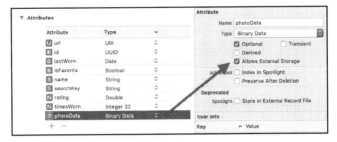

When you enable **Allows External Storage**, Core Data heuristically decides on a per-value basis if it should save the data directly in the database or store a URI that points to a separate file.

> **Note:** The **Allows External Storage** option is only available for the binary data attribute type. In addition, if you turn it on, you won't be able to query Core Data using this attribute.

In summary, besides Strings, Integers, Doubles, Booleans and Dates, Core Data can also save Binary Data, and it can do so efficiently and intelligently.

Storing non-standard data types in Core Data

Still, there are many other types of data you may want to save. For example, what would you do if you had to store an instance of `UIColor`?

With the options presented so far, you'd have to deconstruct the color into its individual components and save them as integers (e.g., red: 255, green: 101, blue: 155). Then, after fetching these components, you'd have to reconstitute your color at runtime.

Alternatively, you could serialize the `UIColor` instance to `Data` and save it as binary data. Then again, you'd also have to "add water" afterward to reconstitute the binary data back to the `UIColor` object you wanted in the first place.

Once again, Core Data has your back. If you took a close look at **SampleData.plist**, you probably noticed each bow tie has an associated color. Select the `BowTie` entity in the model editor and add a new attribute named **tintColor** of data type **Transformable**.

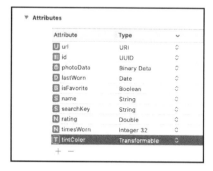

You can save any data type to Core Data (even ones you define) using the `Transformable` type as long as your type conforms to the `NSCoding` protocol.

`UIColor` conforms to `NSSecureCoding`, which inherits from `NSCoding`, so it can use the transformable type out of the box. If you wanted to save your own custom object, you'd first have to implement the `NSCoding` protocol.

> **Note:** The NSCoding protocol (not to be confused with Swift's Codable protocol) is a simple way to archive and unarchive objects that descend from NSObject into data buffers so they can be saved to disk.

Your data model is now complete. The BowTie entity has the ten attributes it needs to store all the information in **SampleData.plist**.

Managed object subclasses

In the sample project from the last chapter, you used key-value coding to access the attributes on the Person entity. It looked similar to the following:

```
// Set the name
person.setValue(aName, forKeyPath: "name")

// Get the name
let name = person.value(forKeyPath: "name")
```

Even though you can do everything directly on NSManagedObject using key-value coding, that doesn't mean you should!

The biggest problem with key-value coding is you're accessing data using strings instead of strongly-typed classes. This is often jokingly referred to as writing stringly typed code.

As you probably know from experience, stringly typed code is vulnerable to silly human errors such as mistyping and misspelling. Key-value coding also doesn't take full advantage of Swift's type-checking and Xcode's auto-completion. "There must be another way!" you may be thinking, and you're right.

The best alternative to key-value coding is to create NSManagedObject subclasses for each entity in your data model. That means there will be a BowTie class with correct types for each property.

Xcode can generate the subclass for you either manually or automatically. Why would you want Xcode to do it for you? It can be a bit of a hassle having to generate these subclass files and have them clutter up your project if you never have to look at them or change them. Since Xcode 8, you can choose, on a per-entity basis, to have Xcode automatically generate and update these files, and store them in the derived data folder for your project.

This setting is in the **Codegen** field of the **Data Model** inspector when using the model editor. Because you're learning about Core Data in this book, you're not going to use automatic code generation because it helps a lot to be able to easily see the files that have been generated for you.

Make sure you still have **BowTies.xcdatamodeld** open, select the `BowTie` entity and open the Data Model inspector. Set the **Codegen** dropdown to **Manual/None**, as shown below:

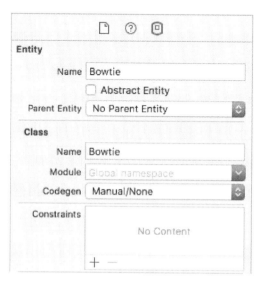

> **Note:** Make sure you change this code generation setting **before** your first compilation, after you add the `BowTie` entity to the model.
>
> If you set the code generation setting *after* your first compilation, you'll have two versions of the managed object subclass: one in derived data, and a second one in your source code. If this happens, you'll run into problems when you try to compile again.

Now go to **Editor\Create NSManagedObject Subclass...**. Select the data model and then the `BowTie` entity in the next two dialog boxes. Click **Create** to save the file.

Xcode generated two Swift files for you, one called **BowTie+CoreDataClass.swift** and a second called **BowTie+CoreDataProperties.swift**. Open **BowTie+CoreDataClass.swift**. It should look like this:

```
import Foundation
import CoreData
```

```
@objc(BowTie)
public class BowTie: NSManagedObject {

}
```

Next, open **BowTie+CoreDataProperties.swift**. Your generated properties may not be in the same order as shown here, but the file should look similar to the following:

```
import Foundation
import CoreData

extension BowTie {

  @nonobjc public class func fetchRequest()
    -> NSFetchRequest<BowTie> {

    return NSFetchRequest<BowTie>(entityName: "BowTie")
  }

  @NSManaged public var name: String?
  @NSManaged public var isFavorite: Bool
  @NSManaged public var lastWorn: Date?
  @NSManaged public var rating: Double
  @NSManaged public var searchKey: String?
  @NSManaged public var timesWorn: Int32
  @NSManaged public var id: UUID?
  @NSManaged public var url: URL?
  @NSManaged public var photoData: Data?
  @NSManaged public var tintColor: NSObject?
}
```

In object-oriented parlance, an object is a set of **values** along with a set of **operations** defined on those values. In this case, Xcode separates these two things into two separate files. The values (i.e. the properties that correspond to the BowTie attributes in your data model) are in **BowTie+CoreDataProperties.swift**, whereas the operations are in the currently empty **BowTie+CoreDataClass.swift**.

> **Note:** If your BowTie entity changes, you can go to **Editor\Create NSManagedObject Subclass...** one more time to re-generate **BowTie+CoreDataProperties.swift**. The second time you do this, you won't re-generate **BowTie+CoreDataClass.swift**, so no overwriting any methods you added there. In fact, this is the primary reason why Core Data generates two files, instead of generating one as it used to do in previous versions of Xcode.

Xcode has created a class with a property for each attribute in your data model.

There is a corresponding class in Foundation or in the Swift standard library for every attribute type in the model editor. Here's the full mapping of attribute types to runtime classes:

- **String** maps to String?

- **Integer 16** maps to Int16

- **Integer 32** maps to Int32

- **Integer 64** maps to Int64

- **Float** maps to Float

- **Double** maps to Double

- **Boolean** maps to Bool

- **Decimal** maps to NSDecimalNumber?

- **Date** maps to Date?

- **URI** maps to URL?

- **UUID** maps to UUID?

- **Binary data** maps to Data?

- **Transformable** maps to NSObject?

> **Note:** Similar to @dynamic in Objective-C, the @NSManaged attribute informs the Swift compiler that the backing store and implementation of a property will be provided at runtime instead of compile time.
>
> The normal pattern is for a property to be backed by an instance variable in memory. A property on a managed object is different: It's backed by the managed object context, so the source of the data is not known at compile time.

Congratulations, you've just made your first managed object subclass in Swift!

Compared with key-value coding, this is a much better way of working with Core Data entities and has two main benefits:

1. Managed object subclasses unleash the syntactic power of Swift properties. By accessing attributes using properties instead of key-value coding, you befriend Xcode and the compiler.

2. You gain the ability to override existing methods or to add your own. Note there are some NSManagedObject methods you must never override. Check Apple's documentation of NSManagedObject for a complete list.

To make sure everything is hooked up correctly between the data model and your new managed object subclass, you'll perform a small test.

Open **AppDelegate.swift** and replace application(_:didFinishLaunchingWithOptions:) with the following implementation:

```swift
func application(_ application: UIApplication,
                didFinishLaunchingWithOptions
  launchOptions: [UIApplication.LaunchOptionsKey: Any]?)
                -> Bool {

  // Save test bow tie
  let bowtie = NSEntityDescription.insertNewObject(
    forEntityName: "BowTie",
    into: self.persistentContainer.viewContext) as! BowTie
  bowtie.name = "My bow tie"
  bowtie.lastWorn = Date()
  saveContext()

  // Retrieve test bow tie
  let request: NSFetchRequest<BowTie> = BowTie.fetchRequest()

  if let ties =
    try? self.persistentContainer.viewContext.fetch(request),
    let testName = ties.first?.name,
    let testLastWorn = ties.first?.lastWorn {
    print("Name: \(testName), Worn: \(testLastWorn)")
  } else {
    print("Test failed.")
  }

  return true
}
```

On app launch, this test creates a bow tie and sets its name and lastWorn properties before saving the managed object context. Immediately after that, it fetches all BowTie entities and prints the name and the lastWorn date of the first one to the console; there should only be one at this point. Build and run the application and pay close attention to the console:

```
Name: My bow tie, Worn: 2019-07-28 03:00:28 +0000
```

If you've been following along carefully, name and lastWorn print to the console as expected. This means you were able to save and fetch a BowTie managed object subclass successfully. With this new knowledge under your belt, it's time to implement the entire sample app.

Propagating a managed context

Open **ViewController.swift** and add the following below import UIKit:

```
import CoreData
```

Next, add the following below the last IBOutlet property:

```
// MARK: - Properties
var managedContext: NSManagedObjectContext!
```

To reiterate, before you can do anything in Core Data, you first have to get an NSManagedObjectContext to work with. Knowing how to **propagate** a managed object context to different parts of your app is an important aspect of Core Data programming.

Open **AppDelegate.swift** and replace application(_:didFinishLaunchingWithOptions:), which currently contains the test code, with the following implementation:

```
func application(_ application: UIApplication,
                 didFinishLaunchingWithOptions
  launchOptions: [UIApplication.LaunchOptionsKey: Any]?)
  -> Bool {
  return true
}
```

You've got seven bow ties dying to enter your Core Data store. Open **ViewController.swift** and add the following method below rate(_:):

```
// Insert sample data
  func insertSampleData() {

    let fetch: NSFetchRequest<BowTie> = BowTie.fetchRequest()
```

```
    fetch.predicate = NSPredicate(format: "searchKey != nil")

    let count = try! managedContext.count(for: fetch)

    if count > 0 {
      // SampleData.plist data already in Core Data
      return
    }
    let path = Bundle.main.path(forResource: "SampleData",
                                ofType: "plist")
    let dataArray = NSArray(contentsOfFile: path!)!

    for dict in dataArray {
      let entity = NSEntityDescription.entity(
        forEntityName: "BowTie",
        in: managedContext)!
      let bowtie = BowTie(entity: entity,
                          insertInto: managedContext)
      let btDict = dict as! [String: Any]

      bowtie.id = UUID(uuidString: btDict["id"] as! String)
      bowtie.name = btDict["name"] as? String
      bowtie.searchKey = btDict["searchKey"] as? String
      bowtie.rating = btDict["rating"] as! Double
      let colorDict = btDict["tintColor"] as! [String: Any]
      bowtie.tintColor = UIColor.color(dict: colorDict)

      let imageName = btDict["imageName"] as? String
      let image = UIImage(named: imageName!)
      bowtie.photoData = image?.pngData()
      bowtie.lastWorn = btDict["lastWorn"] as? Date

      let timesNumber = btDict["timesWorn"] as! NSNumber
      bowtie.timesWorn = timesNumber.int32Value
      bowtie.isFavorite = btDict["isFavorite"] as! Bool
      bowtie.url = URL(string: btDict["url"] as! String)
    }
    try! managedContext.save()
  }
```

Xcode will complain about a missing method declaration on `UIColor`. To fix this, add the following private `UIColor` extension to the end of the file below the last curly brace.

```
private extension UIColor {

  static func color(dict: [String : Any]) -> UIColor? {

    guard let red = dict["red"] as? NSNumber,
      let green = dict["green"] as? NSNumber,
      let blue = dict["blue"] as? NSNumber else {
```

```
        return nil
    }

    return UIColor(red: CGFloat(truncating: red) / 255.0,
                 green: CGFloat(truncating: green) / 255.0,
                 blue: CGFloat(truncating: blue) / 255.0,
                 alpha: 1)
  }
}
```

That's quite a bit of code, but it's all relatively straightforward. The first method, `insertSampleData`, checks for any bow ties; you'll learn how this works later. If none are present, it grabs the bow tie information in **SampleData.plist**, iterates through each bow tie dictionary and inserts a new `BowTie` entity into your Core Data store. At the end of this iteration, it saves the managed object context property to commit these changes to disk.

The `color(dict:)` method you added to `UIColor` via private extension is also simple. **SampleData.plist** stores colors in a dictionary containing three keys: `red`, `green` and `blue`. This static method takes in this dictionary and returns a bona fide `UIColor`.

There are two things here to make special note of:

1. **The way you store images in Core Data.** The property list contains a file name for each bow tie, not the file image — the actual images are in the project's asset catalog. With this file name, you instantiate the `UIImage` and immediately convert it into `Data` by means of `pngData()` before storing it in the `imageData` property.

2. **The way you store the color.** Even though the color is stored in a transformable attribute, it doesn't require any special treatment before you store it in `tintColor`. You simply set the property and you're good to go.

The previous methods insert all the bow tie data you had in **SampleData.plist** into Core Data. Now you need to access the data from somewhere!

Next, replace `viewDidLoad()` with the following implementation:

```
// MARK: - View Life Cycle
override func viewDidLoad() {
  super.viewDidLoad()

  let appDelegate =
    UIApplication.shared.delegate as? AppDelegate
  managedContext = appDelegate?.persistentContainer.viewContext
```

```
//1
insertSampleData()

//2
let request: NSFetchRequest<BowTie> = BowTie.fetchRequest()
let firstTitle = segmentedControl.titleForSegment(at: 0)!
request.predicate = NSPredicate(
  format: "%K = %@",
  argumentArray: [#keyPath(BowTie.searchKey), firstTitle])

do {
  //3
  let results = try managedContext.fetch(request)

  //4
  populate(bowtie: results.first!)
} catch let error as NSError {
  print("Could not fetch \(error), \(error.userInfo)")
}
}
```

This is where you fetch the bow ties from Core Data and populate the UI.

Step by step, here's what you're doing with this code:

1. You call `insertSampleData()`, which you implemented earlier. Since `viewDidLoad()` can be called every time the app is launched, `insertSampleData()` performs a fetch to make sure it isn't inserting the sample data into Core Data multiple times.

2. You create a fetch request for the purpose of fetching the newly inserted `BowTie` entities. The segmented control has tabs to filter by color, so the predicate adds the condition to find the bow ties matching the selected color. Predicates are both very flexible and very powerful — you'll read more about them in Chapter 4, "Intermediate Fetching."

    For now, know this particular predicate is looking for bow ties with their `searchKey` property set to the segmented control's first button title: in this case, **R**.

3. As always, the managed object context does the heavy lifting for you. It executes the fetch request you crafted moments earlier and returns an array of `BowTie` objects.

4. You populate the user interface with the first bow tie in the `results` array. If there was an error, print the error to the console.

You haven't defined the populate method yet, so Xcode is throwing a warning. Add the following implementation below insertSampleData():

```swift
func populate(bowtie: BowTie) {

  guard let imageData = bowtie.photoData as Data?,
    let lastWorn = bowtie.lastWorn as Date?,
    let tintColor = bowtie.tintColor as? UIColor else {
      return
  }

  imageView.image = UIImage(data: imageData)
  nameLabel.text = bowtie.name
  ratingLabel.text = "Rating: \(bowtie.rating)/5"

  timesWornLabel.text = "# times worn: \(bowtie.timesWorn)"

  let dateFormatter = DateFormatter()
  dateFormatter.dateStyle = .short
  dateFormatter.timeStyle = .none

  lastWornLabel.text =
    "Last worn: " + dateFormatter.string(from: lastWorn)

  favoriteLabel.isHidden = !bowtie.isFavorite
  view.tintColor = tintColor
}
```

There's a UI element for most attributes defined in a bow tie. Since Core Data only stores the image as a blob of binary data, it's your job to reconstitute it back into an image so the view controller's image view can use it.

Similarly, you can't use the lastWorn date attribute directly. You first need to create a date formatter to turn the date into a string humans can understand.

Finally, the tintColor transformable attribute that stores your bow tie's color changes the color of not one, but all the elements on the screen. Simply set the tint color on the view controller's view and *voilà*! Everything is now tinted the same color.

> **Note**: Xcode generates some NSManagedObject subclass properties as optional types. That's why inside the populate method, you unwrap some of the Core Data properties on BowTie using a guard statement at the beginning of the method.

Build and run the app. The red bow tie appears on the screen, like so:

The **Wear** and **Rate** buttons do nothing at the moment. Tapping on the different parts of the segmented controls also does nothing. You've still got work to do!

First, you need to keep track of the currently selected bow tie so you can reference it from anywhere in your class. Still in **ViewController.swift**, add the following property below `managedContext` to do this:

```
var currentBowTie: BowTie!
```

Next, replace the `do-catch` statement in `viewDidLoad()` with the following to use `currentBowTie`:

```
do {
  let results = try managedContext.fetch(request)
  currentBowTie = results.first

  populate(bowtie: results.first!)
} catch let error as NSError {
  print("Could not fetch \(error), \(error.userInfo)")
}
```

Keeping track of the currently selected bow tie is necessary to implement the **Wear** and **Rate** buttons since these actions only affect the current bow tie.

Every time the user taps on **Wear**, the button executes the wear(_:) action method. But wear(_:) is empty at the moment. Replace the wear(_:) implementation with the following:

```swift
@IBAction func wear(_ sender: UIButton) {

  let times = currentBowTie.timesWorn
  currentBowTie.timesWorn = times + 1
  currentBowTie.lastWorn = Date()

  do {
    try managedContext.save()
    populate(bowtie: currentBowTie)
  } catch let error as NSError {
    print("Could not fetch \(error), \(error.userInfo)")
  }
}
```

This method takes the currently selected bow tie and increments its timesWorn attribute by one. Next, you change the lastWorn date to today and save the managed object context to commit these changes to disk. Finally, you populate the user interface to visualize these changes.

Build and run the application and tap **Wear** as many times as you'd like. It looks like you thoroughly enjoy the timeless elegance of a red bow tie!

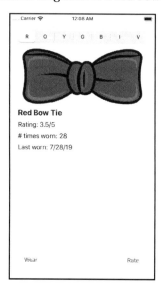

Similarly, every time the user taps on **Rate**, it executes the rate(_:) action method in your code. rate(_:) is currently empty. Replace the implementation of rate(_:) with the following:

```
@IBAction func rate(_ sender: UIButton) {

  let alert = UIAlertController(title: "New Rating",
                                message: "Rate this bow tie",
                                preferredStyle: .alert)

  alert.addTextField { (textField) in
    textField.keyboardType = .decimalPad
  }

  let cancelAction = UIAlertAction(title: "Cancel",
                                   style: .cancel)

  let saveAction = UIAlertAction(title: "Save",
                                 style: .default) {
    [unowned self] action in

    if let textField = alert.textFields?.first {
      self.update(rating: textField.text)
    }
  }

  alert.addAction(cancelAction)
  alert.addAction(saveAction)

  present(alert, animated: true)
}
```

Tapping on **Rate** now brings up an alert view controller with a single text field, a cancel button and a save button. Tapping the save button calls update(rating:), which...

Whoops, you haven't defined that method yet. Appease Xcode by adding the following implementation below populate(bowtie:):

```
func update(rating: String?) {

  guard let ratingString = rating,
    let rating = Double(ratingString) else {
      return
  }

  do {
    currentBowTie.rating = rating
    try managedContext.save()
    populate(bowtie: currentBowTie)
```

```
    } catch let error as NSError {
      print("Could not save \(error), \(error.userInfo)")
    }
  }
```

You convert the text from the alert view's text field into a Double and use it to update the current bow ties rating property. Finally, you commit your changes as usual by saving the managed object context and refresh the UI to see your changes in real time.

Try it out. Build and run the app and tap **Rate**:

Enter any decimal number from 0 to 5 and tap **Save**. As you'd expect, the rating label updates to the new value you entered. Now tap **Rate** one more time. Remember the timeless elegance of a red bow tie? Let's say you like it so much you decide to rate it a 6 out of 5. Tap **Save** to refresh the user interface:

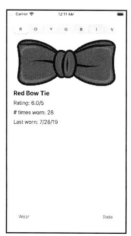

While you may absolutely *love* the color red, this is neither the time nor the place for hyperbole. Your app let you save a 6 for a value that's only supposed to go up to 5. You've got invalid data on your hands.

Data validation in Core Data

Your first instinct may be to write client-side validation—something like, "Only save the new rating if the value is greater than 0 and less than 5." Fortunately, you don't have to write this code yourself. Core Data supports validation for most attribute types out of the box.

Open **BowTies.xcdatamodeld**, select the **rating** attribute and open the data model inspector.

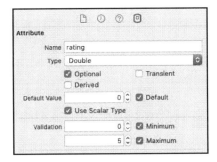

Next to **Validation**, type **0** for minimum and **5** for maximum. That's it! No need to write any Swift to reject invalid data.

> **Note**: Normally, you have to **version** your data model if you want to change it after you've shipped your app. You'll learn more about this in Chapter 6, "Versioning and Migration."
>
> Attribute validation is one of the few exceptions. If you add it to your app after shipping, you don't have to version your data model. Lucky you!

But what does this do, exactly?

Validation kicks in immediately after you call save() on your managed object context. The managed object context checks with the model to see if any of the new values conflict with the validation rules you've put in place.

If there's a validation error, the save fails. Remember that `NSError` in the `do-catch` block wrapping the `save` method? Up until now, you've had no reason to do anything special if there's an error other than log it to the console. Validation changes that.

Build and run the app once more. Give the red bowtie a rating of 6 out of 5 and save. A rather cryptic error message will spill out onto your console:

```
Could not save Error Domain=NSCocoaErrorDomain Code=1610 "rating
is too large." UserInfo={NSValidationErrorObject=<BowTie:
0x600002b8ab20> (entity: BowTie; id: 0xcef31f910384f2ad <x-
coredata://A64812B6-5D4D-4934-805C-72F6A345EC7B/BowTie/p5>;
data: {
    id = "800C3526-E83A-44AC-B718-D36934708921";
    isFavorite = 0;
    lastWorn = "2019-07-28 04:08:02 +0000";
    name = "Red Bow Tie";
    photoData = "{length = 50, bytes = 0x89504e47 0d0a1a0a
0000000d 49484452 ... aece1ce9 00000078 }";
    rating = 6;
    searchKey = R;
    timesWorn = 28;
    tintColor = "UIExtendedSRGBColorSpace 0.937255 0.188235
0.141176 1";
    url = "https://en.wikipedia.org/wiki/Bow_tie";
}), NSLocalizedDescription=rating is too large.,
NSValidationErrorKey=rating, NSValidationErrorValue=6},
["NSValidationErrorKey": rating, "NSLocalizedDescription":
rating is too large., "NSValidationErrorValue": 6,
"NSValidationErrorObject": <BowTie: 0x600002b8ab20> (entity:
BowTie; id: 0xcef31f910384f2ad <x-coredata://
A64812B6-5D4D-4934-805C-72F6A345EC7B/BowTie/p5>; data: {
    id = "800C3526-E83A-44AC-B718-D36934708921";
    isFavorite = 0;
    lastWorn = "2019-07-28 04:08:02 +0000";
    name = "Red Bow Tie";
    photoData = "{length = 50, bytes = 0x89504e47 0d0a1a0a
0000000d 49484452 ... aece1ce9 00000078 }";
    rating = 6;
    searchKey = R;
    timesWorn = 28;
    tintColor = "UIExtendedSRGBColorSpace 0.937255 0.188235
0.141176 1";
    url = "https://en.wikipedia.org/wiki/Bow_tie";
})]
```

The `userInfo` dictionary that comes with the error contains all kinds of useful information about why Core Data aborted your save operation. It even has a localized error message you can show your users, under the key `NSLocalizedDescription`: `rating is too large.`

What you do with this error, however, is entirely up to you. Open
ViewController.swift and replace update(rating:) with the following to handle
the error appropriately:

```
func update(rating: String?) {

  guard let ratingString = rating,
    let rating = Double(ratingString) else {
      return
  }

  do {

    currentBowTie.rating = rating
    try managedContext.save()
    populate(bowtie: currentBowTie)

  } catch let error as NSError {

    if error.domain == NSCocoaErrorDomain &&
      (error.code == NSValidationNumberTooLargeError ||
        error.code == NSValidationNumberTooSmallError) {
      rate(rateButton)
    } else {
      print("Could not save \(error), \(error.userInfo)")
    }
  }
}
```

If there's an error that occurred because the new rating was either too large or too
small, then you present the alert view again.

Otherwise, you populate the user interface with the new rating as before.

But wait... Where did NSValidationNumberTooLargeError and
NSValidationNumberTooSmallError come from? Go back to the previous console
reading and look closely at the first line:

```
Could not save Error Domain=NSCocoaErrorDomain Code=1610 "rating
is too large."
```

NSValidationNumberTooLargeError is an error code that maps to the integer 1610.

For a full list of Core Data errors and code definitions, you can consult
CoreDataErrors.h in Xcode by Control-Cmd-clicking on
NSValidationNumberTooLargeError.

Note: When an NSError is involved, it's standard practice to check the domain and code for the error to determine what went wrong. You can read more about this in Apple's Error Handling Programming Guide:https://developer.apple.com/library/archive/documentation/Cocoa/Conceptual/ErrorHandlingCocoa/CreateCustomizeNSError/CreateCustomizeNSError.html

Build and run the app. Verify the new validation rules work properly by once again showing the red tie some love.

If you enter any value above 5 and try to save, the app rejects your rating and asks you to try again with a new alert view. Success!

Tying everything up

The **Wear** and **Rate** buttons are working properly, but the app can only display one
tie. Tapping the different values on the segmented control is supposed to switch ties.
You'll finish up this sample project by implementing that feature.

Every time the user taps the segmented control, it executes the
segmentedControl(_:) action method in your code. Replace the implementation of
segmentedControl(_:) with the following:

```
@IBAction func segmentedControl(_ sender: UISegmentedControl) {
  guard let selectedValue = sender.titleForSegment(
    at: sender.selectedSegmentIndex) else {
      return
  }

  let request: NSFetchRequest<BowTie> = BowTie.fetchRequest()
  request.predicate = NSPredicate(
    format: "%K = %@",
    argumentArray: [#keyPath(BowTie.searchKey), selectedValue])

  do {
    let results =  try managedContext.fetch(request)
    currentBowTie =  results.first
    populate(bowtie: currentBowTie)

  } catch let error as NSError {
    print("Could not fetch \(error), \(error.userInfo)")
  }
}
```

The title of each segment in the segmented control corresponds to a particular tie's
searchKey attribute. Grab the title of the currently selected segment and fetch the
appropriate bow tie using a well-crafted NSPredicate.

Then, use the first bow tie in the array of results (there should only be one per
searchKey) to populate the user interface.

Build and run the app. Tap different letters on the segmented control for a psychedelic treat.

You did it! With this bow tie app under your belt, you're well on your way to becoming a Core Data master.

Key points

- Core Data supports different **attribute data types**, which determines the kind of data you can store in your entities and how much space they will occupy on disk. Some common attribute data types are **String**, **Date**, and **Double**.

- The **Binary Data** attribute data type gives you the option of storing arbitrary amounts of binary data in your data model.

- The **Transformable** attribute data type lets you store any object that conforms to NSCoding in your data model.

- Using an NSManagedObject **subclass** is a better way to work with a Core Data entity. You can either generate the subclass manually or let Xcode do it automatically.

- You can **refine** the set entities fetched by NSFetchRequest using an NSPredicate.

- You can set **validation rules** (e.g. maximum value and minimum value) to most attribute data types directly in the data model editor. The managed object context will throw an error if you try to save invalid data.

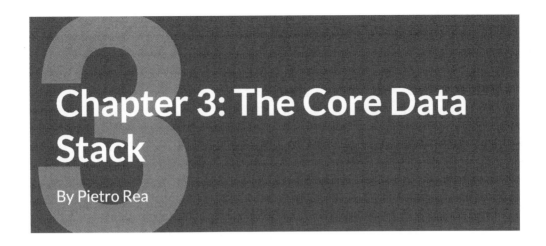

Chapter 3: The Core Data Stack

By Pietro Rea

Until now, you've been relying on Xcode's Core Data template. There's nothing wrong with getting help from Xcode (that's what it's there for!). But if you really want to know how Core Data works, building your own Core Data stack is a must.

The stack is made up of four Core Data classes:

- NSManagedObjectModel
- NSPersistentStore
- NSPersistentStoreCoordinator
- NSManagedObjectContext

Of these four classes, you've only encountered NSManagedObjectContext so far in this book. But the other three were there behind the scenes the whole time, supporting your managed context.

In this chapter, you'll learn the details of what these four classes do. Rather than rely on the default starter template, you'll build your own Core Data stack: a customizable **wrapper** around these classes.

Getting started

The sample project for this chapter is a simple dog-walking app. This application lets you save the date and time of your dog walks in a simple table view. Use this app regularly and your pooch (and his bladder) will love you.

You'll find the sample project **DogWalk** in the resources accompanying this book. Open **DogWalk.xcodeproj**, then build and run the starter project.

As you can see, the sample app is already a fully-working (albeit simple) prototype. Tapping on the plus (+) button on the top-right adds a new entry to the list of walks. The image represents the dog you're currently walking, but otherwise does nothing.

The app has all the functionality it needs, except for one important feature: The list of walks doesn't persist. If you terminate **DogWalk** and re-launch, your entire history is gone. How will you remember if you walked your pooch this morning?

Your task in this chapter is to save the list of walks in Core Data. If that sounds like something you've already done in Chapters 1 and 2, here's the twist: you'll be writing your own Core Data stack to understand what's really going on under the hood!

Rolling your own Core Data stack

Knowing how the Core Data stack works is more than a **nice to know**. If you're working with a more advanced setup, such as migrating data from an old persistent store, digging into the stack is essential.

Before you jump into the code, let's consider what each of the four classes in the Core Data stack — NSManagedObjectModel, NSPersistentStore, NSPersistentStoreCoordinator and NSManagedObjectContext — does in detail.

> **Note**: This is one of the few parts of the book where you'll read about the theory before using the concepts in practice. It's almost impossible to separate one component from the rest of the stack and use it in isolation.

The managed object model

The NSManagedObjectModel represents each object type in your app's data model, the properties they can have, and the relationships between them. Other parts of the Core Data stack use the model to create objects, store properties and save data.

As mentioned earlier in the book, it can be helpful to think about NSManagedObjectModel as a database schema. If your Core Data stack uses SQLite under the hood, NSManagedObjectModel represents the schema for the database.

However, SQLite is only one of many persistent store types you can use in Core Data (more on this later), so it's better to think of the managed object model in more general terms.

> **Note**: You may be wondering how NSManagedObjectModel relates to the data model editor you've been using all along. Good question!
>
> The visual editor creates and edits an **xcdatamodel** file. There's a special compiler, momc, that compiles the model file into a set of files in a **momd** folder.
>
> Just as your Swift code is compiled and optimized so it can run on a device, the compiled model can be accessed efficiently at runtime. Core Data uses the compiled contents of the **momd** folder to initialize an NSManagedObjectModel at runtime.

The persistent store

NSPersistentStore reads and writes data to whichever storage method you've decided to use. Core Data provides four types of NSPersistentStore out of the box: three atomic and one non-atomic.

An **atomic** persistent store needs to be completely deserialized and loaded into memory before you can make any read or write operations. In contrast, a **non-atomic** persistent store can load chunks of itself onto memory as needed.

Here's a brief overview of the four built-in Core Data store types:

1. **NSSQLiteStoreType** is backed by an SQLite database. It's the only non-atomic store type Core Data supports out of the box, giving it a lightweight and efficient memory footprint. This makes it the best choice for most iOS projects. Xcode's Core Data template uses this store type by default.

2. **NSXMLStoreType** is backed by an XML file, making it the most human-readable of all the store types. This store type is atomic, so it can have a large memory footprint. NSXMLStoreType is only available on OS X.

3. **NSBinaryStoreType** is backed by a binary data file. Like NSXMLStoreType, it's also an atomic store, so the entire binary file must be loaded onto memory before you can do anything with it. You'll rarely find this type of persistent store in real-world applications.

4. **NSInMemoryStoreType** is the in-memory persistent store type. In a way, this store type is not really *persistent*. Terminate the app or turn off your phone, and the data stored in an in-memory store type disappears into thin air. Although this may seem to defeat the purpose of Core Data, in-memory persistent stores can be helpful for unit testing and some types of caching.

> **Note**: Were you holding your breath for a persistent store type backed by a JSON file or a CSV file? Bummer. The good news is you can create your own type of persistent store by subclassing NSIncrementalStore.
>
> Refer to Apple's Incremental Store Programming Guide if you're curious about this option:
>
> https://developer.apple.com/library/ios/documentation/DataManagement/Conceptual/IncrementalStorePG/Introduction/Introduction.html

The persistent store coordinator

NSPersistentStoreCoordinator is the bridge between the managed object model and the persistent store. It's responsible for using the model and the persistent stores to do most of the hard work in Core Data. It understands the NSManagedObjectModel and knows how to send information to, and fetch information from, the NSPersistentStore.

NSPersistentStoreCoordinator also hides the implementation details of how your persistent store or stores are configured. This is useful for two reasons:

1. NSManagedObjectContext (coming next!) doesn't have to know if it's saving to an SQLite database, XML file or even a custom incremental store.

2. If you have multiple persistent stores, the persistent store coordinator presents a unified interface to the managed context. As far as the managed context is concerned, it always interacts with a single, aggregate persistent store.

The managed object context

On a day-to-day basis, you'll work with NSManagedObjectContext the most out of the four stack components. You'll probably only see the other three components when you need to do something more advanced with Core Data.

Since working with NSManagedObjectContext is so common, understanding how contexts work is very important! Here are some things you may have already picked up from the book so far:

- A context is an in-memory scratchpad for working with your managed objects.

- You do all of the work with your Core Data objects within a managed object context.

- Any changes you make won't affect the underlying data on disk until you call save() on the context.

Now here are five things about contexts not mentioned before. A few of them are very important for later chapters, so pay close attention:

1. The context *manages* the lifecycle of the objects it creates or fetches. This lifecycle management includes powerful features such as faulting, inverse relationship handling and validation.

2. A managed object cannot exist without an associated context. In fact, a managed object and its context are so tightly coupled that every managed object keeps a reference to its context, which can be accessed like so:

```
let managedContext = employee.managedObjectContext
```

3. Contexts are very territorial; once a managed object has been associated with a particular context, it will remain associated with the same context for the duration of its lifecycle.

4. An application can use more than one context — most non-trivial Core Data applications fall into this category. Since a context is an in-memory scratch pad for what's on disk, you can actually load the same Core Data object onto two different contexts simultaneously.

5. A context is not thread-safe. The same goes for a managed object: You can only interact with contexts and managed objects on the same thread in which they were created.

Apple has provided many ways to work with contexts in multithreaded applications. You'll read all about different concurrency models in Chapter 9, "Multiple Managed Object Contexts."

The persistent store container

If you thought there were only four pieces to the Core Data stack, you're in for a suprise! As of iOS 10, there's a new class to orchestrate all four Core Data stack classes: the managed model, the store coordinator, the persistent store and the managed context.

The name of this class is `NSPersistentContainer` and as its name implies, it's a container that holds everything together. Instead of wasting your time writing boilerplate code to wire up all four stack components together, you can simply initialize an `NSPersistentContainer`, load its persistent stores, and you're good to go.

Creating your stack object

Now you know what each component does, it's time to return to **DogWalk** and implement your own Core Data stack.

As you know from previous chapters, Xcode creates its Core Data stack in the app delegate. You're going to do it differently. Instead of mixing app delegate code with Core Data code, you'll create a separate class to encapsulate the stack.

Go to **File ▸ New ▸ File...**, select the **iOS ▸ Source ▸ Swift File** template and click **Next**. Name the file **CoreDataStack** and click **Create** to save the file.

Go to the newly created **CoreDataStack.swift**. You'll be creating this file piece-by-piece. Start by replacing the contents of the file with the following:

```swift
import Foundation
import CoreData

class CoreDataStack {

  private let modelName: String

  init(modelName: String) {
    self.modelName = modelName
  }

  private lazy var storeContainer: NSPersistentContainer = {

    let container = NSPersistentContainer(name: self.modelName)
    container.loadPersistentStores {
      (storeDescription, error) in
      if let error = error as NSError? {
        print("Unresolved error \(error), \(error.userInfo)")
      }
    }
    return container
  }()
}
```

You start by importing the Foundation and CoreData modules. Next, create a private property to store the modelName. Next, create an initializer to save modelName into private property.

Next, you set up a lazily instantiated NSPersistentContainer, passing the modelName you stored during initialization. The only other thing you need to do is call loadPersistentStores(completionHandler:) on the persistent container (despite the appearance of the completion handler, this method doesn't run asynchronously by default). Finally, add the following lazily instantiated property below modelName:

```swift
lazy var managedContext: NSManagedObjectContext = {
  return self.storeContainer.viewContext
}()
```

Even though `NSPersistentContainer` has public accessors for its managed context, the managed model, the store coordinator and the persistent stores (via `[NSPersistentStoreDescription]`), `CoreDataStack` works a bit differently.

For instance, the only publicly accessible part of `CoreDataStack` is the `NSManagedObjectContext` because of the lazy property you just added. Everything else is marked `private`. Why is this?

The managed context is the only entry point required to access the rest of the stack. The persistent store coordinator is a public property on the `NSManagedObjectContext`. Similarly, both the managed object model and the array of persistent stores are public properties on the `NSPersistentStoreCoordinator`.

Finally, add the following method below the `storeContainer` property:

```
func saveContext () {
  guard managedContext.hasChanges else { return }

  do {
    try managedContext.save()
  } catch let error as NSError {
    print("Unresolved error \(error), \(error.userInfo)")
  }
}
```

This is a convenience method to save the stack's managed object context and handle any resulting errors.

Open **ViewController.swift** and make the following changes. First, import the Core Data module below `import UIKit`:

```
import CoreData
```

Next, add the following property below `dateFormatter` to hold the Core Data stack:

```
lazy var coreDataStack = CoreDataStack(modelName: "DogWalk")
```

Modeling your data

Now your shiny new Core Data stack is securely fastened to the main view controller, it's time to create your data model.

Head over to your Project Navigator and… Wait a second. There's no data model file! That's right. Since you generated this sample application without enabling the option to use Core Data, there's no **.xcdatamodeld** file.

No worries. Go to **File ▸ New ▸ File…**, select the **iOS ▸ Core Data ▸ Data Model** template and click **Next**.

Name the file **DogWalk.xcdatamodeld** and click **Create** to save the file.

Note: You'll have problems later on if you don't name your data model file precisely **DogWalk.xcdatamodeld**. This is because **CoreDataStack.swift** expects to find the compiled version at **DogWalk.momd.**

Open the data model file and create a new entity named **Dog**. You should be able to do this on your own by now, but in case you forgot how, click the **Add Entity** button on the bottom left.

Add an attribute named **name** of type **String**. Your data model should look like this:

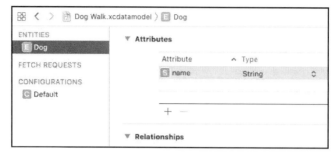

You also want to keep track of the walks for a particular dog. After all, that's the whole point of the app!

Define another entity and name it **Walk**. Then add an attribute named **date** and set its type to **Date**.

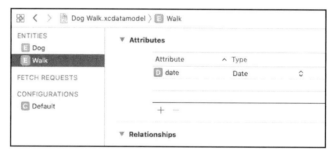

Go back to the Dog entity. You might think you need to add a new attribute of type **Array** to hold the walks, but there is no array type in Core Data. Instead, the way to do this is to model it as a relationship. Add a new relationship and name it **walks**. Set the destination to **Walk**:

You can think of the destination as the receiving end of a relationship. Every relationship begins as a to-one relationship by default, which means you can only track one walk per dog at the moment. Unless you don't plan on keeping your dog for very long, you probably want to track more than one walk.

To fix this, with the **walks** relationship selected, open the **Data Model** Inspector:

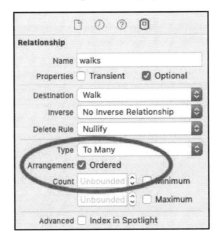

Click on the **Type** dropdown, select **To Many** and check **Ordered**. This means one dog can have many walks and the order of the walks matters, since you'll be displaying the walks sorted by date.

Select the **Walk** entity and create an inverse relationship back to **Dog**. Set the destination as **dog** and the inverse as **walks**.

It's OK to leave this relationship as a to-one relationship. A dog can have many walks, but a walk can only belong to one dog — for the purposes of this app, at least.

The inverse lets the model know how to find its way back, so to speak. Given a walk record, you can follow the relationship to the dog. Thanks to the inverse, the model knows to follow the **walks** relationship to get back to the walk record.

This is a good time to let you know the data model editor has another view style. This entire time you've been looking at the table editor style.

Toggle the segmented control on the bottom-right to switch to the graph editor style:

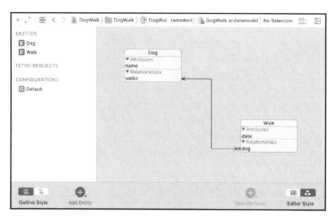

The graph editor is a great tool to visualize the relationships between your Core Data entities. Here the to-many relationship from Dog to Walk is represented with a double arrow. Walk points back to Dog with a single arrow, indicating a to-one relationship.

Feel free to switch back and forth between the two editor styles. You might find it easier to use the table style to add and remove entities and attributes, and the graph style to see the big picture of your data model.

Adding managed object subclasses

In the previous chapter, you learned how to create custom managed object subclasses for your Core Data entities. It's more convenient to work this way, so this is what you'll do for Dog and Walk as well.

Like in the previous chapter, you're going to generate custom managed object subclasses manually instead of letting Xcode do it for you so you can see what's going on behind the scenes. Open **DogWalk.xcdatamodeld**, select the Dog entity and set the **Codegen** dropdown in the Data Model inspector to **Manual/None**. Repeat the same process for the Walk entity.

Then, go to **Editor ▸ Create NSManagedObject Subclass...** and choose the **DogWalk** model, and then both the **Dog** and **Walk** entities. Click **Create** on the next screen to create the files.

As you saw in Chapter 2, doing this creates two files per entity: one for the Core Data properties you defined in the model editor and one for any future functionality you may add to your managed object subclass.

Dog+CoreDataProperties.swift should look like this:

```swift
import Foundation
import CoreData

extension Dog {

  @nonobjc public class func fetchRequest()
    -> NSFetchRequest<Dog> {
    return NSFetchRequest<Dog>(entityName: "Dog")
  }

  @NSManaged public var name: String?
  @NSManaged public var walks: NSOrderedSet?
}

// MARK: Generated accessors for walks
extension Dog {

  @objc(insertObject:inWalksAtIndex:)
  @NSManaged public func insertIntoWalks(_ value: Walk,
                                         at idx: Int)

  @objc(removeObjectFromWalksAtIndex:)
  @NSManaged public func removeFromWalks(at idx: Int)

  @objc(insertWalks:atIndexes:)
  @NSManaged public func insertIntoWalks(_ values: [Walk],
                                         at indexes: NSIndexSet)

  @objc(removeWalksAtIndexes:)
  @NSManaged public func removeFromWalks(at indexes: NSIndexSet)

  @objc(replaceObjectInWalksAtIndex:withObject:)
  @NSManaged public func replaceWalks(at idx: Int,
                                      with value: Walk)

  @objc(replaceWalksAtIndexes:withWalks:)
  @NSManaged public func replaceWalks(at indexes: NSIndexSet,
                                      with values: [Walk])

  @objc(addWalksObject:)
  @NSManaged public func addToWalks(_ value: Walk)

  @objc(removeWalksObject:)
  @NSManaged public func removeFromWalks(_ value: Walk)

  @objc(addWalks:)
```

```
    @NSManaged public func addToWalks(_ values: NSOrderedSet)

    @objc(removeWalks:)
    @NSManaged public func removeFromWalks(_ values: NSOrderedSet)
}
```

Like before, the name attribute is a String optional. But what about the walks relationship? Core Data represents to-many relationships using sets, not arrays. Because you made the walks relationship ordered, you've got an NSOrderedSet.

> **Note**: NSSet seems like an odd choice, doesn't it? Unlike arrays, sets don't allow accessing their members by index. In fact, there's no ordering at all! Core Data uses NSSet because a set forces uniqueness among its members. The same object can't feature more than once in a to-many relationship.
>
> If you need to access individual objects by index, you can check the **Ordered** checkbox in the visual editor, as you've done here. Core Data will then represent the relationship as an NSOrderedSet.

Similarly, **Walk+CoreDataProperties.swift** should look like this:

```
import Foundation
import CoreData

extension Walk {

  @nonobjc public class func fetchRequest()
    -> NSFetchRequest<Walk> {
    return NSFetchRequest<Walk>(entityName: "Walk")
  }

  @NSManaged public var date: Date?
  @NSManaged public var dog: Dog?
}
```

The inverse relationship back to Dog is simply a property of type Dog. Easy as pie.

> **Note**: Sometimes Xcode will create relationship properties with the generic NSManagedObject type instead of the specific class, especially if you're making lots of subclasses at the same time. If this happens, just correct the type yourself or generate the specific file again.

A walk down persistence lane

Now your setup is complete: your Core Data stack, your data model and your managed object subclasses. It's time to convert **DogWalk** to use Core Data. You've done this several times before, so this should be an easy section for you.

Pretend for a moment this application will at some point support tracking multiple dogs. The first step is to track the currently selected dog.

Open **ViewController.swift** and replace the walks array with the following property. Ignore the errors for now, you'll fix those in a minute:

```
var currentDog: Dog?
```

Next, add the following code to the end of viewDidLoad():

```
let dogName = "Fido"
let dogFetch: NSFetchRequest<Dog> = Dog.fetchRequest()
dogFetch.predicate = NSPredicate(format: "%K == %@",
                                #keyPath(Dog.name), dogName)

do {
  let results = try coreDataStack.managedContext.fetch(dogFetch)
  if results.count > 0 {
    // Fido found, use Fido
    currentDog = results.first
  } else {
    // Fido not found, create Fido
    currentDog = Dog(context: coreDataStack.managedContext)
    currentDog?.name = dogName
    coreDataStack.saveContext()
  }
} catch let error as NSError {
  print("Fetch error: \(error) description: \(error.userInfo)")
}
```

First, you fetch all Dog entities with names of "Fido" from Core Data. You'll learn more about fancy fetch requests like this in the next chapter.

If the fetch request came back with results, you set the first entity (there should only be one) as the currently selected dog.

If the fetch request comes back with zero results, this probably means it's the user's first time opening the app. If this is the case, you insert a new dog, name it "Fido", and set it as the currently selected dog.

> **Note**: You've just implemented what's often referred to as the **Find or Create** pattern. The purpose of this pattern is to manipulate an object stored in Core Data without running the risk of adding a duplicate object in the process. In iOS 9, Apple introduced the ability to specify **unique constraints** on your Core Data entities. With unique constraints, you can specify in your data model which attributes must always be unique on an entity to avoid adding duplicates.

Next, replace the implementation of `tableView(_:numberOfRowsInSection:)` with the following:

```
func tableView(_ tableView: UITableView,
               numberOfRowsInSection section: Int) -> Int {

  return currentDog?.walks?.count ?? 0
}
```

As you can probably guess, this ties the number of rows in the table view to the number of walks set in the currently selected dog. If there is no currently selected dog, return 0.

Next, replace `tableView(_:cellForRowAt:)` with the following:

```
func tableView(_ tableView: UITableView,
               cellForRowAt indexPath: IndexPath)
               -> UITableViewCell {

  let cell =
    tableView.dequeueReusableCell(withIdentifier: "Cell",
                                  for: indexPath)

  guard let walk = currentDog?.walks?[indexPath.row] as? Walk,
    let walkDate = walk.date as Date? else {
      return cell
  }

  cell.textLabel?.text = dateFormatter.string(from: walkDate)
  return cell
}
```

Only two lines of code have changed. Now, you take the date of each walk and display it in the corresponding table view cell.

The add(_:) method still has a reference to the old walks array. Comment it out for now; you'll re-implement this method in the next step:

```
@IBAction func add(_ sender: UIBarButtonItem) {
  // walks.append(Date())
  tableView.reloadData()
}
```

Build and run to make sure you have everything hooked up correctly.

Hooray! If you've gotten this far, you've just inserted a dog into Core Data and are currently populating the table view with his list of walks. This list doesn't have any walks at the moment, so the table doesn't look very exciting.

Tap the plus (+) button, and it understandably does nothing. You haven't implemented anything underneath this control yet! Before transitioning to Core Data, add(_:) simply added a Date to an array and reloaded the table view. Re-implement it as shown below:

```
@IBAction func add(_ sender: UIBarButtonItem) {

  // Insert a new Walk entity into Core Data

  let walk = Walk(context: coreDataStack.managedContext)
  walk.date = Date()

  // Insert the new Walk into the Dog's walks set

  if let dog = currentDog,
```

```
    let walks = dog.walks?.mutableCopy()
                     as? NSMutableOrderedSet {
      walks.add(walk)
      dog.walks = walks
    }

    // Save the managed object context

    coreDataStack.saveContext()

    // Reload table view

    tableView.reloadData()
  }
```

The Core Data version of this method is much more complicated. First, you have to create a new `Walk` entity and set its `date` attribute to now. Next, you have to insert this walk into the currently selected dog's list of walks.

However, the walks attribute is of type `NSOrderedSet`. `NSOrderedSet` is immutable, so you first have to create a mutable copy (`NSMutableOrderedSet`), insert the new walk and then reset an immutable copy of this mutable ordered set back on the dog.

Note: Is adding a new object into a to-many relationship making your head spin? Many people can sympathize, which is why **Dog+CoreDataProperties** contains generated accessors to the `walks` ordered set that will handle all of this for you.

For example, you can replace the entire `if-let` statement in the last code snippet with the following:

```
currentDog?.addToWalks(walk)
```

Give it a try!

Core Data can make things easier for you, though. If the relationship weren't ordered, you'd just be able to set the one side of the relationship (e.g., walk.dog = currentDog) rather than the many side and Core Data would use the inverse relationship defined in the model editor to add the walk to the dog's set of walks.

Finally, you commit your changes to the persistent store by calling `saveContext()` on the Core Data stack and you reload the table view.

Build and run the app, and tap the plus (+) button a few times.

Great! The list of walks should now be saved in Core Data. Verify this by terminating the app in the fast app switcher and re-launching from scratch.

Deleting objects from Core Data

Let's say you were too trigger-friendly and tapped the plus (+) button when you didn't mean to. You didn't actually walk your dog, so you want to delete the walk you just added.

You've added objects to Core Data, you've fetched them, modified them and saved them again. What you haven't done yet is delete them — but you're about to do that next.

First, open **ViewController.swift** and add the following method to the UITableViewDataSource extension:

```
func tableView(_ tableView: UITableView,
                canEditRowAt indexPath: IndexPath) -> Bool {
```

```
    return true
}
```

You're going to use UITableView's default behavior for deleting items: swipe left to reveal the red **Delete** button, then tap on it to delete.

The table view calls this UITableViewDataSource method to ask if a particular cell is editable, and returning true means all the cells should be editable.

Next, add the following method to the same UITableViewDataSource extension:

```
func tableView(_ tableView: UITableView,
               commit editingStyle:
UITableViewCell.EditingStyle,
               forRowAt indexPath: IndexPath) {

  //1
  guard let walkToRemove =
    currentDog?.walks?[indexPath.row] as? Walk,
    editingStyle == .delete else {
      return                      .
  }

  //2
  coreDataStack.managedContext.delete(walkToRemove)

  //3
  coreDataStack.saveContext()

  //4
  tableView.deleteRows(at: [indexPath], with: .automatic)
}
```

This table view data source method is called when you tap the red **Delete** button. Let's go through the code step-by-step:

1. First, you get a reference to the walk you want to delete.

2. Remove the walk from Core Data by calling NSManagedObjectContext's delete() method. Core Data also takes care of removing the deleted walk from the current dog's walks relationship.

3. No changes are final until you save your managed object context — not even deletions!

4. Finally, if the save operation succeeds, you animate the table view to tell the user about the deletion.

Build and run the app one more time. You should have several walks from previous runs. Pick any and swipe to the left.

Tap on the Delete button to remove the walk. Verify that the walk is actually gone by terminating the app and re-launching from scratch. The walk you just removed is gone for good. Core Data giveth and Core Data taketh away.

> **Note**: Deleting used to be one of the most "dangerous" Core Data operations. Why is this? When you remove something from Core Data, you have to delete *both* the record on disk as well as any outstanding references in code.
>
> Trying to access an `NSManagedObject` that had no Core Data backing store resulted in the the much-feared `inaccessible fault` Core Data crash.
>
> Starting with iOS 9, deletion is safer than ever. Apple introduced the property `shouldDeleteInaccessibleFaults` on `NSManagedObjectContext`, which is turned on by default. This marks bad faults as deleted and treats missing data as `NULL/nil/0`.

Key points

- The **Core Data stack** is made up of five classes: `NSManagedObjectModel`, `NSPersistentStore`, `NSPersistentStoreCoordinator`, `NSManagedObjectContext` and the `NSPersistentContainer` that holds everything together.

- The **managed object model** represents each object type in your app's data model, the properties they can have, and the relationship between them.

- A **persistent store** can be backed by a SQLite database (the default), XML, a binary file or in-memory store. You can also provide your own backing store with the **incremental store** API.

- The **persistent store coordinator** hides the implementation details of how your persistent stores are configured and presents a simple interface for your **managed object context**.

- The **managed object context** manages the lifecycles of the managed objects it creates or fetches. They are responsible for fetching, editing and deleting managed objects, as well as more powerful features such as validation, faulting and inverse relationship handling.

Chapter 4: Intermediate Fetching

By Pietro Rea

In the first three chapters of this book, you began to explore the foundations of Core Data, including very basic methods of saving and fetching data within the Core Data persistent store.

To this point, you've mostly performed simple, unrefined fetches such as "fetch all BowTie entities." Sometimes this is all you need to do. Often, you'll want to exert more control over how you retrieve information from Core Data.

Building on what you've learned so far, this chapter dives deep into the topic of **fetching**. Fetching is a large topic in Core Data, and you have many tools at your disposal. By the end of this chapter, you'll know how to:

- Fetch only what you need to

- Refine your fetched results using predicates

- Fetch in the background to avoid blocking the UI

- Avoid unnecessary fetching by updating objects directly in the persistent store

This chapter is a toolbox sampler; its aim is to expose you to many fetching techniques, so that when the time comes, you'll know what tool to use.

NSFetchRequest: the star of the show

As you've learned in previous chapters, you fetch records from Core Data by creating an instance of NSFetchRequest, configuring it as you like and handing it over to NSManagedObjectContext to do the heavy lifting.

Seems simple enough, but there are actually **five** different ways to get hold of a fetch request. Some are more popular than others, but you'll likely encounter all of them at some point as a Core Data developer.

Before jumping to the starter project for this chapter, here are the five different ways to set up a fetch request so you're not caught by surprise:

```
// 1
let fetchRequest1 = NSFetchRequest<Venue>()
let entity =
  NSEntityDescription.entity(forEntityName: "Venue",
                             in: managedContext)!
fetchRequest1.entity = entity

// 2
let fetchRequest2 = NSFetchRequest<Venue>(entityName: "Venue")

// 3
let fetchRequest3: NSFetchRequest<Venue> = Venue.fetchRequest()

// 4
let fetchRequest4 =
  managedObjectModel.fetchRequestTemplate(forName: "venueFR")

// 5
let fetchRequest5 =
  managedObjectModel.fetchRequestFromTemplate(
    withName: "venueFR",
    substitutionVariables: ["NAME" : "Vivi Bubble Tea"])
```

Going through each in turn:

1. You initialize an instance of NSFetchRequest as generic type: NSFetchRequest<Venue>. At a minimum, you must specify a NSEntityDescription for the fetch request. In this case, the entity is Venue. You initialize an instance of NSEntityDescription and use it to set the fetch request's entity property.

2. Here you use NSFetchRequest's convenience initializer. It initializes a new fetch request and sets its entity property in one step. You simply need to provide a string for the entity name rather than a full-fledged NSEntityDescription.

3. Just as the second example was a contraction of the first, the third is a contraction of the second. When you generate an NSManagedObject subclass, this step also generates a class method that returns an NSFetchRequest already set up to fetch corresponding entity types. This is where Venue.fetchRequest() comes from. This code lives in **Venue+CoreDataProperties.swift**.

4. In the fourth example, you retrieve your fetch request from your NSManagedObjectModel. You can configure and store commonly used fetch requests in Xcode's data model editor. You'll learn how to do this later in the chapter.

5. The last case is similar to the fourth. Retrieve a fetch request from your managed object model, but this time, you pass in some extra variables. These "substitution" variables are used in a predicate to refine your fetched results.

The first three examples are the simple cases you've already seen. You'll see even more of these simple cases in the rest of this chapter, in addition to stored fetch requests and other tricks of NSFetchRequest!

> **Note**: If you're not already familiar with it, NSFetchRequest is a generic type. If you inspect NSFetchRequest's initializer, you'll notice it takes in type as a parameter <ResultType : NSFetchRequestResult>.
>
> ResultType specifies the type of objects you **expect** as a result of the fetch request. For example, if you're expecting an array of Venue objects, the result of the fetch request is now going to be [Venue] instead of [Any]. This is helpful because you don't have to cast down to [Venue] anymore.

Introducing the BubbleTea app

This chapter's sample project is a bubble tea app. For those of you who don't know about bubble tea (also known as "boba tea"), it's a Taiwanese tea-based drink containing large tapioca pearls. It's very yummy!

You can think of this bubble tea app as an ultra-niche Yelp. Using the app, you can find locations near you selling your favorite Taiwanese drink.

For this chapter, you'll only be working with static venue data from Foursquare: that's about 30 locations in New York City that sell bubble tea. You'll use this data to build the filter/sort screen to arrange the list of static venues as you see fit.

Go to this chapter's files and open **BubbleTeaFinder.xcodeproj**. Build and run the starter project.

You'll see the following:

The sample app consists of a number of table view cells with static information. Although the sample project isn't very exciting at the moment, there's a lot of setup already done for you.

Open the project navigator and take a look at the full list of files in the starter project:

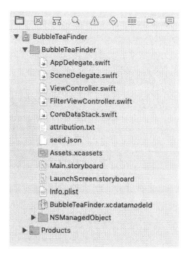

It turns out most of the Core Data setup you had to do in the first section of the book comes ready for you to use. Below is a quick overview of the components you get in the starter project, grouped into categories:

- **Seed data: seed.json** is a JSON file containing real-world venue data for venues in New York City serving bubble tea. Since this is real data coming from Foursquare, the structure is more complex than previous seed data used in this book.

- **Data model:** Click on **BubbleTeaFinder.xcdatamodeld** to open Xcode's model editor. The most important entity is Venue. It contains attributes for a venue's name, phone number and the number of specials it's offering at the moment.

   Since the JSON data is rather complex, the data model breaks down a venue's information into other entities. These are Category, Location, PriceInfo and Stats. For example, Location has attributes for city, state, country, and others.

- **Managed object subclasses:** All the entities in your data model also have corresponding NSManagedObject subclasses. These are **Venue+CoreDataClass.swift**, **Location+CoreDataClass.swift**, **PriceInfo+CoreDataClass.swift**, **Category+CoreDataClass.swift** and **Stats+CoreDataClass.swift**. You can find these in the **NSManagedObject** group along with their accompanying **EntityName+CoreDataProperties.swift** file.

- **CoreDataStack**: As in previous chapters, this object wraps an NSPersistentStoreContainer object, which itself contains the cadre of Core Data objects known as the "stack": the context, the model, the persistent store and the persistent store coordinator. No need to set this up — it comes ready-to-use.

- **View Controllers:** The initial view controller that shows you the list of venues is **ViewController.swift**. On first launch, the initial view controller reads from **seed.json**, creates corresponding Core Data objects and saves them to the persistent store. Tapping the **Filter** button on the top-right brings up **FilterViewController.swift**. There's not much going on here at the moment. You'll add code to these two files throughout this chapter.

When you first launched the sample app, you saw only static information. However, your app delegate had already read the seed data from **seed.json**, parsed it into Core Data objects and saved them into the persistent store.

Your first task will be to fetch this data and display it in the table view. This time, you'll do it with a twist.

Stored fetch requests

As previously mentioned, you can store frequently used fetch requests right in the data model. Not only does this make them easier to access, but you also get the benefit of using a GUI-based tool to set up the fetch request parameters.

Open **BubbleTeaFinder.xcdatamodeld** and long-click the **Add Entity** button:

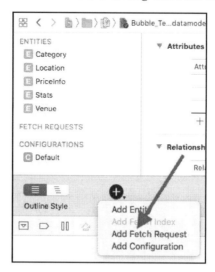

Select **Add Fetch Request** from the menu. This will create a new fetch request on the left-side bar and take you to a special fetch request editor:

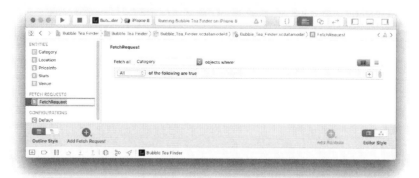

Note: You can click on the newly created fetch request on the left-hand sidebar to change its name.

You can make your fetch request as general or as specific as you want using the visual tool in Xcode's data model editor. To start, create a fetch request that retrieves all Venue objects from the persistent store.

You only need to make one change here: click the dropdown menu next to **Fetch all** and select **Venue**.

That's all you need to do. If you wanted to refine your fetch request with an additional predicate, you could also add conditions from the fetch request editor.

Time to take your newly created fetch request out for a spin. Open **ViewController.swift** and add the following two properties below `coreDataStack`:

```
var fetchRequest: NSFetchRequest<Venue>?
var venues: [Venue] = []
```

The first property will hold your fetch request. The second property is the array of Venue objects you'll use to populate the table view.

Next, add the following to the end of `viewDidLoad()`:

```
guard let model =
  coreDataStack.managedContext
    .persistentStoreCoordinator?.managedObjectModel,
  let fetchRequest = model
    .fetchRequestTemplate(forName: "FetchRequest")
    as? NSFetchRequest<Venue> else {
      return
  }

self.fetchRequest = fetchRequest
fetchAndReload()
```

Doing this connects the `fetchRequest` property you just set up to the one you created using Xcode's data model editor. There are three things to remember here:

1. Unlike other ways of getting a fetch request, this one involves the managed object model. This is why you must go through the `coreDataStack` property to retrieve your fetch request.

2. As you saw in the previous chapter, you constructed `CoreDataStack` so only the managed context is public. To retrieve the managed object model, you have to go through the managed context's persistent store coordinator.

3. `NSManagedObjectModel`'s `fetchRequestTemplate(forName:)` takes a string identifier. This identifier must exactly match the name you chose for your fetch request in the model editor. Otherwise, your app will throw an exception and crash.

The last line calls a method you haven't defined yet, so Xcode will complain about it. To fix that, add the following extension above the `UITableViewDataSource` extension:

```
// MARK: - Helper methods
extension ViewController {

  func fetchAndReload() {

    guard let fetchRequest = fetchRequest else {
      return
    }

    do {
      venues =
        try coreDataStack.managedContext.fetch(fetchRequest)
      tableView.reloadData()
    } catch let error as NSError {
      print("Could not fetch \(error), \(error.userInfo)")
    }
  }
}
```

As its name suggests, `fetchAndReload()` executes the fetch request and reloads the table view. Other methods in this class will need to see the fetched objects, so you store the fetched results in the `venues` property you defined earlier.

There's one more thing you have to do before you can run the sample project: hook up the table view's data source with the fetched Venue objects.

In the `UITableViewDataSource` extension, replace the placeholder implementations of `tableView(_:numberOfRowsInSection:)` and `tableView(_:cellForRowAt:)` with the following:

```
func tableView(_ tableView: UITableView,
               numberOfRowsInSection section: Int) -> Int {
  return venues.count
}
```

```swift
func tableView(_ tableView: UITableView,
               cellForRowAt indexPath: IndexPath)
         -> UITableViewCell {

  let cell =
    tableView.dequeueReusableCell(
      withIdentifier: venueCellIdentifier, for: indexPath)

  let venue = venues[indexPath.row]
  cell.textLabel?.text = venue.name
  cell.detailTextLabel?.text = venue.priceInfo?.priceCategory
  return cell
}
```

You've implemented these methods many times in this book, so you're probably familiar with what they do. The first method, `tableView(_:numberOfRowsInSection:)`, matches the number of cells in the table view with the number of fetched objects in the `venues` array.

The second method, `tableView(_:cellForRowAt:)`, dequeues a cell for a given index path and populates it with the information of the corresponding Venue in the `venues` array. In this case, the main label gets the venue's name and the detail label gets a price category that is one of three possible values: **$, $$** or **$$$**.

Build and run the project, and you'll see the following:

Scroll down the list of bubble tea venues. These are all real places in New York City that sell the delicious drink.

> **Note**: When should you store fetch requests in your data model?
>
> If you know you'll be making the same fetch over and over in different parts of your app, you can use this feature to save you from writing the same code multiple times. A drawback of stored fetch requests is that there is no way to specify a sort order for the results. Therefore, the list of venues you saw may have been in a different order than in the book.

Fetching different result types

All this time, you've probably been thinking of NSFetchRequest as a fairly simple tool. You give it some instructions and you get some objects in return. What else is there to it?

If this is the case, you've been underestimating this class. NSFetchRequest is the multi-function Swiss army knife of the Core Data framework!

You can use it to fetch individual values, compute statistics on your data such as the average, minimum, maximum, and more.

How is this possible, you ask? NSFetchRequest has a property named resultType. So far, you've only used the default value, .managedObjectResultType. Here are all the possible values for a fetch request's resultType:

- **.managedObjectResultType:** Returns managed objects (default value).

- **.countResultType**: Returns the count of the objects matching the fetch request.

- **.dictionaryResultType**: This is a catch-all return type for returning the results of different calculations.

- **.managedObjectIDResultType**: Returns unique identifiers instead of full-fledged managed objects.

Let's go back to the sample project and apply these concepts in practice.

With the sample project running, tap **Filter** in the top-right corner to bring up the UI for the filter screen.

You won't implement the actual filters or sorts right now. Instead, you'll focus on the following four labels:

The filter screen is divided into three sections: **Price**, **Most Popular** and **Sort By**. That last section is not technically made up of "filters", but sorting usually goes hand-in-hand with filters, so you'll leave it like that.

Below each price filter is space for the total number of venues that fall into that price category. Similarly, there's a spot for the total number of deals across all venues. You'll implement these next.

Returning a count

Open **FilterViewController.swift** and add the following below import UIKit:

```
import CoreData
```

Next, add the following property below the last @IBOutlet property:

```
// MARK: - Properties
var coreDataStack: CoreDataStack!
```

This will hold a reference to the `CoreDataStack` object you've been using in
ViewController.swift.

Next, open **ViewController.swift** and replace the `prepare(for:sender:)`
implementation with the following:

```
override func prepare(for segue: UIStoryboardSegue,
                      sender: Any?) {

  guard segue.identifier == filterViewControllerSegueIdentifier,
    let navController = segue.destination
      as? UINavigationController,
    let filterVC = navController.topViewController
      as? FilterViewController else {
        return
  }

  filterVC.coreDataStack = coreDataStack
}
```

The new line of code propagates the `CoreDataStack` object from `ViewController` to
`FilterViewController`. The filter screen is now ready to use Core Data.

Open **FilterViewController.swift** and add the following lazy property below
`coreDataStack`:

```
lazy var cheapVenuePredicate: NSPredicate = {
  return NSPredicate(format: "%K == %@",
    #keyPath(Venue.priceInfo.priceCategory), "$")
}()
```

You'll use this lazily-instantiated `NSPredicate` to calculate the number of venues in
the lowest price category.

> **Note**: `NSPredicate` supports string-based key paths. This is why you can drill
> down from the `Venue` entity into the `PriceInfo` entity using
> `priceInfo.priceCategory`, and use the `#keyPath` keyword to get safe,
> compile-time checked values for the key path.
>
> As of this writing, `NSPredicate` does not support Swift 4 style key paths such
> as `\Venue.priceInfo.priceCategory`.

Next, add the following extension below the `UITableViewDelegate` extension:

```
// MARK: - Helper methods
extension FilterViewController {

  func populateCheapVenueCountLabel() {

    let fetchRequest =
      NSFetchRequest<NSNumber>(entityName: "Venue")
    fetchRequest.resultType = .countResultType
    fetchRequest.predicate = cheapVenuePredicate

    do {
      let countResult =
        try coreDataStack.managedContext.fetch(fetchRequest)

      let count = countResult.first!.intValue
      let pluralized = count == 1 ? "place" : "places"
      firstPriceCategoryLabel.text =
        "\(count) bubble tea \(pluralized)"
    } catch let error as NSError {
      print("count not fetched \(error), \(error.userInfo)")
    }
  }
}
```

This extension provides `populateCheapVenueCountLabel()` which creates a fetch request to fetch Venue entities. You then set the result type to `.countResultType` and set the fetch request's `predicate` to `cheapVenuePredicate`. Notice that for this to work correctly, the fetch request's type parameter has to be `NSNumber`, not Venue.

When you set a fetch result's result type to `.countResultType`, the return value becomes a Swift array containing a single `NSNumber`. The integer inside the `NSNumber` is the total count you're looking for.

Once again, you execute the fetch request against `CoreDataStack`'s `NSManagedObjectContext` property. Then you extract the integer from the resulting `NSNumber` and use it to populate `firstPriceCategoryLabel`.

Before you run the sample app, add the following to the bottom of `viewDidLoad()`:

```
populateCheapVenueCountLabel()
```

Now build and run to test if these changes took effect. Tap **Filter** to bring up the filter/sort menu:

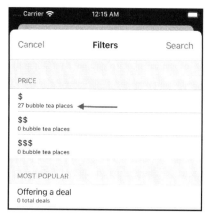

The label under the first price filter now says "27 bubble tea places." Hooray! You've successfully used `NSFetchRequest` to calculate a count.

> **Note**: You may be thinking that you could have just as easily fetched the actual Venue objects and gotten the count from the array's `count` property. That's true. Fetching counts instead of objects is mainly a performance optimization. For example, if you had census data for New York City and wanted to know how many people lived in its metropolitan area, would you prefer Core Data gave you the number 8,300,000 (an integer) or an array of 8,300,000 records?
>
> Obviously, getting the count directly is more memory-efficient. There's a whole chapter devoted to Core Data performance. If you want to learn more about performance optimization in Core Data, check out Chapter 8, "Measuring and Boosting Performance."

Now that you're acquainted with the count result type, you can quickly implement the count for the second price category filter. Add the following lazy property below `cheapVenuePredicate`:

```
lazy var moderateVenuePredicate: NSPredicate = {
  return NSPredicate(format: "%K == %@",
    #keyPath(Venue.priceInfo.priceCategory), "$$")
}()
```

This `NSPredicate` is almost identical to the cheap venue predicate, except this one matches against **$$** instead of **$**. Similarly, add the following method below `populateCheapVenueCountLabel()`:

```
func populateModerateVenueCountLabel() {

  let fetchRequest =
    NSFetchRequest<NSNumber>(entityName: "Venue")
  fetchRequest.resultType = .countResultType
  fetchRequest.predicate = moderateVenuePredicate

  do {

    let countResult =
      try coreDataStack.managedContext.fetch(fetchRequest)

    let count = countResult.first!.intValue
    let pluralized = count == 1 ? "place" : "places"
    secondPriceCategoryLabel.text =
      "\(count) bubble tea \(pluralized)"
  } catch let error as NSError {
    print("count not fetched \(error), \(error.userInfo)")
  }
}
```

Finally, add the following line to the bottom of `viewDidLoad()` to invoke your newly defined method:

```
populateModerateVenueCountLabel()
```

Build and run the sample project. As before, tap **Filter** on the top right to reach the filter/sort screen:

Great news for bubble tea lovers! Only two places are moderately expensive. Bubble tea as a whole seems to be quite accessible.

An alternate way to fetch a count

Now that you're familiar with `.countResultType`, it's a good time to mention that there's an alternate API for fetching a count directly from Core Data.

Since there's one more price category count to implement, you'll use this alternate API now.

Add the follow lazy property below `moderateVenuePredicate`:

```
lazy var expensiveVenuePredicate: NSPredicate = {
  return NSPredicate(format: "%K == %@",
    #keyPath(Venue.priceInfo.priceCategory), "$$$")
}()
```

Next, implement the following method below `populateModerateVenueCountLabel()`:

```
func populateExpensiveVenueCountLabel() {

  let fetchRequest: NSFetchRequest<Venue> = Venue.fetchRequest()
  fetchRequest.predicate = expensiveVenuePredicate

  do {
    let count =
      try coreDataStack.managedContext.count(for: fetchRequest)
    let pluralized = count == 1 ? "place" : "places"
    thirdPriceCategoryLabel.text =
      "\(count) bubble tea \(pluralized)"
  } catch let error as NSError {
    print("count not fetched \(error), \(error.userInfo)")
  }
}
```

Like the previous two scenarios, you create a fetch request for retrieving Venue objects.

Next, you set the predicate that you defined as a lazy property earlier: `expensiveVenuePredicate`.

The difference between this scenario and the last two is that here, you don't set the result type to `.countResultType`. Rather than the usual `fetch(_:)`, you use `NSManagedObjectContext`'s method `count(for:)` instead.

The return value for `count(for:)` is an integer that you can use directly to populate the third price category label. Finally, add the following line to the bottom of `viewDidLoad()` to invoke your newly defined method:

```
populateExpensiveVenueCountLabel()
```

Build and run to see if your latest changes took effect.

The filter/sort screen should look like this:

There's only one bubble tea venue that falls into the **$$$** category. Maybe they use real pearls instead of tapioca?

Performing calculations with fetch requests

All three price category labels are populated with the number of venues that fall into each category. The next step is to populate the label under "Offering a deal." It currently says "0 total deals." That can't be right!

Where exactly does this information come from? Venue has a `specialCount` attribute that captures the number of deals the venue is currently offering. Unlike the labels under the price category, you now need to know the total sum of deals across **all** venues since a particularly savvy venue could have many deals at once.

The naïve approach would be to load all venues into memory and sum their deals using a `for` loop. If you're hoping for a better way, you're in luck: Core Data has built-in support for a number of different functions such as average, sum, min and max.

Open **FilterViewController.swift**, and add the following method below
`populateExpensiveVenueCountLabel()`:

```swift
func populateDealsCountLabel() {

  // 1
  let fetchRequest =
    NSFetchRequest<NSDictionary>(entityName: "Venue")
  fetchRequest.resultType = .dictionaryResultType

  // 2
  let sumExpressionDesc = NSExpressionDescription()
  sumExpressionDesc.name = "sumDeals"

  // 3
  let specialCountExp =
    NSExpression(forKeyPath: #keyPath(Venue.specialCount))
  sumExpressionDesc.expression =
    NSExpression(forFunction: "sum:",
                 arguments: [specialCountExp])
  sumExpressionDesc.expressionResultType =
    .integer32AttributeType

  // 4
  fetchRequest.propertiesToFetch = [sumExpressionDesc]

  // 5
  do {

    let results =
      try coreDataStack.managedContext.fetch(fetchRequest)

    let resultDict = results.first!
    let numDeals = resultDict["sumDeals"] as! Int
    let pluralized = numDeals == 1 ?  "deal" : "deals"
    numDealsLabel.text = "\(numDeals) \(pluralized)"

  } catch let error as NSError {
    print("count not fetched \(error), \(error.userInfo)")
  }
}
```

This method contains a few classes you've not encountered in the book before, so here is each explained in turn:

1. You begin by creating your typical fetch request for retrieving Venue objects. Next, you specify the result type to be `.dictionaryResultType`.

2. You create an `NSExpressionDescription` to request the sum, and give it the name `sumDeals` so you can read its result out of the result dictionary you'll get back from the fetch request.

3. You give the expression description an NSExpression to specify you want the sum function. Next, give **that** expression another NSExpression to specify what property you want to sum over — in this case, specialCount. Finally, you have to set the return data type of your expression description, so you set it to integer32AttributeType.

4. You tell your original fetch request to fetch the sum by setting its propertiesToFetch property to the expression description you just created.

5. Finally, execute the fetch request in the usual do–catch statement. The result type is an NSDictionary array, so you retrieve the result of your expression using your expression description's name (sumDeals) and you're done!

> **Note**: What other functions does Core Data support? To name a few: count, min, max, average, median, mode, absolute value and many more. For a comprehensive list, check out Apple's documentation for NSExpression.

Fetching a calculated value from Core Data requires you to follow many, often unintuitive steps, so make sure you have a good reason for using this technique, such as performance considerations. Finally, add the following line to the bottom of viewDidLoad():

```
populateDealsCountLabel()
```

Build the sample project and open the filter/sort screen to verify your changes.

Great! There are 12 deals across all `venues` stored in Core Data.

You've now used three of the four supported `NSFetchRequest` result types: `.managedObjectResultType`, `.countResultType` and `.dictionaryResultType`.

The remaining result type is `.managedObjectIDResultType`. When you fetch with this type, the result is an array of `NSManagedObjectID` objects rather the actual managed objects they represent. An `NSManagedObjectID` is a compact universal identifier for a managed object. It works like the primary key in the database!

Prior to iOS 5, fetching by ID was popular because `NSManagedObjectID` was thread-safe and using it helped developers implement the thread confinement concurrency model.

Now that thread confinement has been deprecated in favor of more modern concurrency models, there's little reason to fetch by object ID anymore.

> **Note**: You can set up multiple managed object contexts to run concurrent operations and keep long-running operations off the main thread. For more information, check out Chapter 9, "Multiple Managed Object Contexts."

You've gotten a taste of all the things a fetch request can do for you. But just as important as the information a fetch request returns, is the information it **doesn't** return. For practical reasons, you have to cap the incoming data at some point.

Why? Imagine a perfectly connected object graph, one where each Core Data object is connected to every other object through a series of relationships. If Core Data didn't put limits on the information a fetch request returned, you'd be fetching the entire object graph every single time! That's not memory efficient.

You can manually limit the information you get back from a fetch request. For example, `NSFetchRequest` supports fetching batches. You can use the properties `fetchBatchSize`, `fetchLimit` and `fetchOffset` to control the batching behavior.

Core Data also tries to minimize its memory consumption for you by using a technique called **faulting**. A fault is a placeholder object representing a managed object that hasn't yet been fully brought into memory.

Another way to limit your object graph is to use predicates, as you've done to populate the venue count labels above. Let's add the filters to the sample app using predicates.

Open **FilterViewController.swift**, and add the following protocol declaration above your class definition:

```
protocol FilterViewControllerDelegate: class {
  func filterViewController(
    filter: FilterViewController,
    didSelectPredicate predicate: NSPredicate?,
    sortDescriptor: NSSortDescriptor?)
}
```

This protocol defines a delegate method that will notify the delegate when the user selects a new sort/filter combination.

Next, add the following three properties below coreDataStack:

```
weak var delegate: FilterViewControllerDelegate?
var selectedSortDescriptor: NSSortDescriptor?
var selectedPredicate: NSPredicate?
```

This first property will hold a reference to FilterViewController's delegate. It's a weak property instead of a strongly-retained property in order to avoid retain cycles. The second and third properties will hold references to the currently selected NSSortDescriptor and NSPredicate, respectively.

Next, implement search(_:) as shown below:

```
@IBAction func search(_ sender: UIBarButtonItem) {
  delegate?.filterViewController(
    filter: self,
    didSelectPredicate: selectedPredicate,
    sortDescriptor: selectedSortDescriptor)

  dismiss(animated: true)
}
```

This means every time you tap **Search** in the top-right corner of the filter/sort screen, you'll notify the delegate of your selection and dismiss the filter/sort screen to reveal the list of venues behind it.

You need to make one more change in this file. Find tableView(_:didSelectRowAt:) and implement it as shown below:

```
override func tableView(_ tableView: UITableView,
                        didSelectRowAt indexPath: IndexPath) {

  guard let cell = tableView.cellForRow(at: indexPath) else {
    return
  }
```

```
  // Price section
  switch cell {
  case cheapVenueCell:
    selectedPredicate = cheapVenuePredicate
  case moderateVenueCell:
    selectedPredicate = moderateVenuePredicate
  case expensiveVenueCell:
    selectedPredicate = expensiveVenuePredicate
  default: break
  }

  cell.accessoryType = .checkmark
}
```

When the user taps on any of the first three price category cells, this method will map the selected cell to the appropriate predicate. You store a reference to this predicate in selectedPredicate so it's ready when you notify the delegate of the user's selection.

Next, open **ViewController.swift** and add the following extension to conform to the FilterViewControllerDelegate protocol:

```
// MARK: - FilterViewControllerDelegate
extension ViewController: FilterViewControllerDelegate {

  func filterViewController(
    filter: FilterViewController,
    didSelectPredicate predicate: NSPredicate?,
    sortDescriptor: NSSortDescriptor?) {

    guard let fetchRequest = fetchRequest else {
      return
    }

    fetchRequest.predicate = nil
    fetchRequest.sortDescriptors = nil

    fetchRequest.predicate = predicate

    if let sr = sortDescriptor {
      fetchRequest.sortDescriptors = [sr]
    }

    fetchAndReload()
  }
}
```

Adding the FilterViewControllerDelegate Swift extension tells the compiler that this class will conform to this protocol. This delegate method fires every time the user selects a new filter/sort combination.

Here, you reset your fetch request's `predicate` and `sortDescriptors`, then set the predicate and sort descriptor passed into the method and reload the data.

There's one more thing you need to do before you can test your price category filters. Find `prepare(for:sender:)` and add the following line to the end of the method:

```
filterVC.delegate = self
```

This formally sets `ViewController` as `FilterViewController`'s delegate.

Build and run the sample project. Go to the **Filter** screen, tap the first price category cell (**$**) and then tap **Search** in the top-right corner.

Your app crashes with the following error message in the console:

```
2019-08-12 00:31:03.367653-0400 BubbleTeaFinder[19410:4349195]
*** Terminating app due to uncaught exception
'NSInternalInconsistencyException', reason: 'Can't modify a
named fetch request in an immutable model.'
```

What happened? Earlier in the chapter, you defined your fetch request in the data model. It turns out if you use that technique, the fetch request becomes immutable. You can't change its predicate at runtime, or else you'll crash spectacularly. If you want to modify the fetch request in any way, you have to do it in the data model editor in advance.

Open **ViewController.swift**, and replace `viewDidLoad()` with the following:

```
override func viewDidLoad() {
  super.viewDidLoad()

  importJSONSeedDataIfNeeded()

  fetchRequest = Venue.fetchRequest()
  fetchAndReload()
}
```

You removed the lines that retrieves the fetch request from the template in the managed object model. Instead, you get an instance of `NSFetchRequest` directly from the `Venue` entity.

Build and run the sample app one more time. Go to the **Filter** screen, tap the second price category cell (**$$**) and then tap **Search** in the top-right corner.

This is the result:

As expected, there are only two venues in this category. Test the first (**$**) and third (**$ $$**) price category filters as well, making sure the filtered list contains the correct number of venues for each.

You'll practice writing a few more predicates for the remaining filters. The process is similar to what you've done already, so this time you'll do it with less explanation.

Open **FilterViewController.swift** and add these three lazy properties below `expensiveVenuePredicate`:

```
lazy var offeringDealPredicate: NSPredicate = {
  return NSPredicate(format: "%K > 0",
    #keyPath(Venue.specialCount))
}()

lazy var walkingDistancePredicate: NSPredicate = {
  return NSPredicate(format: "%K < 500",
    #keyPath(Venue.location.distance))
}()

lazy var hasUserTipsPredicate: NSPredicate = {
  return NSPredicate(format: "%K > 0",
    #keyPath(Venue.stats.tipCount))
}()
```

The first predicate specifies venues currently offering one or more deals, the second predicate specifies venues less than 500 meters away from your current location and the third predicate specifies venues that have at least one user tip.

> **Note**: So far in the book, you've written predicates with a single condition. You should also know that you can write predicates that check two conditions instead of one by using compound predicate operators such as **AND, OR** and **NOT**.
>
> Alternatively, you can string two simple predicates into one compound predicate by using the class `NSCompoundPredicate`.
>
> `NSPredicate` isn't technically part of Core Data (it's part of `Foundation`) so this book won't cover it in depth, but you can seriously improve your Core Data chops by learning the ins and outs of this nifty class. For more information, make sure to check out Apple's Predicate Programming Guide:
>
> https://developer.apple.com/library/ios/documentation/Cocoa/Conceptual/Predicates/AdditionalChapters/Introduction.html

Next, scroll down to `tableView(_:didSelectRowAt:)`. You're going to add three more cases to the switch statement you added earlier:

```swift
override func tableView(_ tableView: UITableView, didSelectRowAt
  indexPath: IndexPath) {

  guard let cell = tableView.cellForRow(at: indexPath) else {
    return
  }

  switch cell {
  // Price section
  case cheapVenueCell:
    selectedPredicate = cheapVenuePredicate
  case moderateVenueCell:
    selectedPredicate = moderateVenuePredicate
  case expensiveVenueCell:
    selectedPredicate = expensiveVenuePredicate

  // Most Popular section
  case offeringDealCell:
    selectedPredicate = offeringDealPredicate
  case walkingDistanceCell:
    selectedPredicate = walkingDistancePredicate
  case userTipsCell:
    selectedPredicate = hasUserTipsPredicate
```

```
    default: break
    }

    cell.accessoryType = .checkmark
  }
```

Above, you added cases for `offeringDealCell`, `walkingDistanceCell` and `userTipsCell`. These are the three new filters for which you're now adding support.

That's all you need to do. Build and run the sample app. Go to the **Filters** page, select the **Offering a deal** filter and tap **Search**:

You'll see a total of six venues. Note that since you didn't specify a sort descriptor, your list of venues may be in a different order than the venues in the screenshot. You can verify these venues have specials by looking them up in **seed.json**. For example, City Wing Cafe is currently offering four specials. Woo-hoo!

Sorting fetched results

Another powerful feature of `NSFetchRequest` is its ability to sort fetched results for you. It does this by using yet another handy `Foundation` class, `NSSortDescriptor`. These sorts happen at the SQLite level, not in memory. This makes sorting in Core Data fast and efficient.

In this section, you'll implement four different sorts to complete the filter/sort screen.

Open **FilterViewController.swift** and add the following three lazy properties below
`hasUserTipsPredicate`:

```swift
lazy var nameSortDescriptor: NSSortDescriptor = {
  let compareSelector =
    #selector(NSString.localizedStandardCompare(_:))
  return NSSortDescriptor(key: #keyPath(Venue.name),
                          ascending: true,
                          selector: compareSelector)
}()

lazy var distanceSortDescriptor: NSSortDescriptor = {
  return NSSortDescriptor(
    key: #keyPath(Venue.location.distance),
    ascending: true)
}()

lazy var priceSortDescriptor: NSSortDescriptor = {
  return NSSortDescriptor(
    key: #keyPath(Venue.priceInfo.priceCategory),
    ascending: true)
}()
```

The way to add sort descriptors is very similar to the way you added filters. Each sort
descriptor maps to one of these three lazy `NSSortDescriptor` properties.

To initialize an instance of `NSSortDescriptor` you need three things: a key path to
specify the attribute which you want to sort, a specification of whether the sort is
ascending or descending and an optional selector to perform the comparison
operation.

> **Note**: If you've worked with `NSSortDescriptor` before, then you probably
> know there's a block-based API that takes a comparator instead of a selector.
> Unfortunately, Core Data doesn't support this method of defining a sort
> descriptor.
>
> The same thing goes for the block-based method of defining a `NSPredicate`.
> Core Data doesn't support this either. The reason is filtering and sorting
> happens in the SQLite database, so the predicate/sort descriptor has to match
> nicely to something that can be written as an SQL statement.

The three sort descriptors are going to sort by name, distance and price category,
respectively, in ascending order. Before moving on, take a closer look at the first sort
descriptor, `nameSortDescriptor`. The initializer takes in an optional selector,
`NSString.localizedStandardCompare(_:)`. What is that?

Any time you're sorting user-facing strings, Apple recommends that you pass in
`NSString.localizedStandardCompare(_:)` to sort according to the language rules
of the current locale. This means sort will "just work" and do the right thing for
languages with special characters. It's the little things that matter, *bien sûr*!

Next, find `tableView(_:didSelectRowAt:)` and add the following cases to the end
of the `switch` statement above the `default` case:

```
// Sort By section
case nameAZSortCell:
  selectedSortDescriptor = nameSortDescriptor
case nameZASortCell:
  selectedSortDescriptor =
    nameSortDescriptor.reversedSortDescriptor
    as? NSSortDescriptor
case distanceSortCell:
  selectedSortDescriptor = distanceSortDescriptor
case priceSortCell:
  selectedSortDescriptor = priceSortDescriptor
```

Like before, this `switch` statement matches the user tapped cell with the appropriate
sort descriptor, so it's ready to pass to the delegate when the user taps **Search**.

The only wrinkle is the `nameZA` sort descriptor. Rather than creating a separate sort
descriptor, you can reuse the one for A-Z and simply call the method
`reversedSortDescriptor`. How handy!

Everything else is hooked up for you to test the sorts you just implemented. Build
and run the sample app and go to the **Filter** screen. Tap the **Name (Z-A)** sort and
then tap **Search**. You'll see search results ordered like so:

No, you're not seeing double. There really are seven Vivi Bubble Tea venues in the data set — it's a popular bubble tea chain in New York City.

As you scroll down the table view, you'll see the app has indeed sorted the venues alphabetically from Z to A.

You've now completed your **Filter** screen, setting it up so the user can combine any one filter with any one sort. Try different combinations to see what you get. The venue cell doesn't show much information, so if you need to verify a sort, you can go straight to the source and consult **seed.json**.

Asynchronous fetching

If you've reached this point, there's both good news and bad news (and then more good news). The good news is you've learned a lot about what you can do with a plain `NSFetchRequest`. The bad news is that every fetch request you've executed so far has blocked the main thread while you waited for the results to come back.

When you block the main thread, it makes the screen unresponsive to incoming touches and creates a slew of other problems. You haven't felt this blocking of the main thread because you've made simple fetch requests fetching a few objects at a time.

Since the beginning of Core Data, the framework has given developers several techniques to perform fetches in the background. As of iOS 8, Core Data has an API for performing long-running fetch requests in the background and getting a completion callback when the fetch completes.

Let's see this new API in action. Open **ViewController.swift** and add the following property below venues:

```
var asyncFetchRequest: NSAsynchronousFetchRequest<Venue>?
```

There you have it. The class responsible for this asynchronous magic is aptly called `NSAsynchronousFetchRequest`. Don't be fooled by its name, though. It's not directly related to `NSFetchRequest`; it's actually a subclass of `NSPersistentStoreRequest`.

Next, replace the contents of `viewDidLoad()` with the following:

```
override func viewDidLoad() {
  super.viewDidLoad()

  importJSONSeedDataIfNeeded()
```

```
// 1
let venueFetchRequest: NSFetchRequest<Venue> =
  Venue.fetchRequest()
fetchRequest = venueFetchRequest

// 2
asyncFetchRequest =
  NSAsynchronousFetchRequest<Venue>(
  fetchRequest: venueFetchRequest) {
    [unowned self] (result: NSAsynchronousFetchResult) in

    guard let venues = result.finalResult else {
      return
    }

    self.venues = venues
    self.tableView.reloadData()
}

// 3
do {
  guard let asyncFetchRequest = asyncFetchRequest else {
    return
  }
  try coreDataStack.managedContext.execute(asyncFetchRequest)
  // Returns immediately, cancel here if you want
} catch let error as NSError {
  print("Could not fetch \(error), \(error.userInfo)")
}
}
```

There's a lot you haven't seen before, so let's cover it step by step:

1. Notice here that an asynchronous fetch request doesn't replace the regular fetch request. Rather, you can think of an asynchronous fetch request as a *wrapper* around the fetch request you already had.

2. To create an NSAsynchronousFetchRequest you need two things: a plain old NSFetchRequest and a completion handler. Your fetched venues are contained in NSAsynchronousFetchResult's finalResult property. Within the completion handler, you update the venues property and reload the table view.

3. Specifying the completion handler is not enough! You still have to execute the asynchronous fetch request. Once again, CoreDataStack's managedContext property handles the heavy lifting for you. However, notice the method you use is different — this time, it's execute(_:) instead of the usual fetch(_:).

execute(_:) returns immediately. You don't need to do anything with the return value since you're going to update the table view from within the completion block. The return type is NSAsynchronousFetchResult.

> **Note**: As an added bonus to this API, you can cancel the fetch request with NSAsynchronousFetchResult's cancel() method.

Time to see if your asynchronous fetch delivers as promised. If everything goes well, you shouldn't notice any difference in the user interface.

Build and run the sample app, and you should see the list of venues as before:

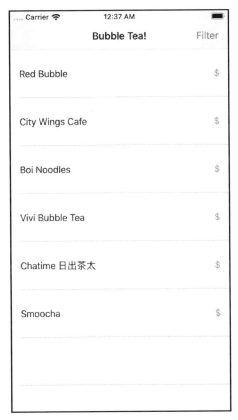

Hooray! You've mastered asynchronous fetching. The filters and sorts will also work, except they still use a plain NSFetchRequest to reload the table view.

Batch updates: no fetching required

Sometimes the only reason you fetch objects from Core Data is to change a single attribute. Then, after you make your changes, you have to commit the Core Data objects back to the persistent store and call it a day. This is the normal process you've been following all along.

But what if you want to update a hundred thousand records all at once? It would take a lot of time and a lot of memory to fetch all of those objects just to update one attribute. No amount of tweaking your fetch request would save your user from having to stare at a spinner for a long, long time.

Luckily, as of iOS 8 there has been new way to update Core Data objects without having to fetch anything into memory: batch updates. This new technique greatly reduces the amount of time and memory required to make those huge kinds of updates.

The new technique bypasses the NSManagedObjectContext and goes straight to the persistent store. The classic use case for batch updates is the "Mark all as read" feature in a messaging application or e-mail client. For this sample app, you're going to do something more fun. Since you love bubble tea so much, you're going to mark every Venue in Core Data as your favorite.

Let's see this in practice. Open **ViewController.swift** and add the following to viewDidLoad() below the importJSONSeedDataIfNeeded() call:

```swift
let batchUpdate = NSBatchUpdateRequest(entityName: "Venue")
batchUpdate.propertiesToUpdate =
  [#keyPath(Venue.favorite): true]

batchUpdate.affectedStores =
  coreDataStack.managedContext
    .persistentStoreCoordinator?.persistentStores

batchUpdate.resultType = .updatedObjectsCountResultType

do {
  let batchResult =
    try coreDataStack.managedContext.execute(batchUpdate)
      as! NSBatchUpdateResult
  print("Records updated \(batchResult.result!)")
} catch let error as NSError {
  print("Could not update \(error), \(error.userInfo)")
}
```

You create an instance of NSBatchUpdateRequest with the entity you want to update, Venue in this case.

Next, you set up your batch update request by setting propertiesToUpdate to a dictionary that contains the key path of the attribute you want to update, favorite, and its new value, true. Then you set affectedStores to your persistent store coordinator's persistentStores array.

Finally, you the result type to return a count and execute your batch update request.

Build and run your sample app. If everything works properly, you'll see the following printed to your console log:

```
Records updated 30
```

Great! You've surreptitiously marked every bubble tea venue in New York City as your favorite.

Now you know how to update your Core Data objects without loading them into memory. Is there another use case where you may want to bypass the managed context and change your Core Data objects directly in the persistent store?

Of course there is — batch deletion!

You shouldn't have to to load objects into memory just to delete them, particularly if you're handling a large number of them. As of iOS 9, you've had NSBatchDeleteRequest for this purpose.

As the name suggests, a batch delete request can efficiently delete a large number Core Data objects in one go.

Like NSBatchUpdateRequest, NSBatchDeleteRequest is also a subclass of NSPersistentStoreRequest. Both types of batch request behave similarly since they both operate directly on the persistent store.

> **Note**: Since you're sidestepping your NSManagedObjectContext, you won't get any validation if you use a batch update request or a batch delete request. Your changes also won't be reflected in your managed context.
>
> Make sure you're sanitizing and validating your data properly before using a persistent store request!

Key Points

- `NSFetchRequest` is a **generic type**. It takes a type parameter that specifies the type of objects you expect to get as the result of the fetch request.

- If you expect to reuse the same type of fetch in different parts of your app, consider using the **Data Model Editor** to store an **immutable** fetch request directly in your data model.

- Use `NSFetchRequest`'s **count** result type to efficiently compute and return counts from SQLite.

- Use `NSFetchRequest`'s **dictionary** result type to efficiently compute and return averages, sums and other common calculations from SQLite.

- A fetch request uses different techniques such as using **batch sizes**, **batch limits** and **faulting** to limit the amount of information returned.

- Add a **sort description** to your fetch request to efficiently sort your fetched results.

- Fetching large amounts of information can block the main thread. Use `NSAsynchronousFetchRequest` to offload some of this work to a background thread.

- `NSBatchUpdateRequest` and `NSBatchDeleteRequest` reduce the amount of time and memory required to update or delete a large number of records in Core Data.

Chapter 5: NSFetchedResultsController

By Pietro Rea

If you followed the previous chapters closely, you probably noticed that most of the sample projects use table views. That's because Core Data fits nicely with table views. Set up your fetch request, fetch an array of managed objects and plug the result into the table view's data source. This is a common, everyday scenario.

If you see a tight relationship between Core Data and UITableView, you're in good company. The authors of the Core Data framework at Apple thought the same way! In fact, they saw *so* much potential for a close connection between UITableView and Core Data they penned a class to formalize this bond: NSFetchedResultsController.

As the name suggests, NSFetchedResultsController is a controller, but it's not a *view* controller. It has no user interface. Its purpose is to make developers' lives easier by abstracting away much of the code needed to synchronize a table view with a data source backed by Core Data.

Set up an NSFetchedResultsController correctly, and your table will "magically" mimic its data source without you have to write more than a few lines of code. In this chapter, you'll learn the ins and outs of this class. You'll also learn when to use it and when not to use it. Are you ready?

Introducing the World Cup app

This chapter's sample project is a World Cup scoreboard app for iOS. On startup, the one-page application will list all the teams contesting for the World Cup. Tapping on a country's cell will increase the country's wins by one. In this simplified version of the World Cup, the country with the most taps wins the tournament. This ranking simplifies the real elimination rules quite a bit, but it's good enough for demonstration purposes.

Go to this chapter's files and find the **starter** folder. Open **WorldCup.xcodeproj**. Build and run the starter project:

The sample application consists of 20 static cells in a table view. Those bright blue boxes are where the teams' flags should be. Instead of real names, you see "Team Name." Although the sample project isn't too exciting, it actually does a lot of the setup for you.

Open the project navigator and take a look at the full list of files in the starter project:

Before jumping into the code, let's briefly go over what each class does for you out of the box. You'll find a lot of the setup you did manually in previous chapters comes already implemented for you. Hooray!

- **CoreDataStack**: As in previous chapters, this object wraps an instance of NSPersistentContainer, which in turn contains the cadre of Core Data objects known as the "stack": the context, the model, the persistent store and the persistent store coordinator. No need to set this up. It comes ready-to-use.

- **ViewController:** The sample project is a one-page application, and this file represents that one page. On first launch, the view controller reads from **seed.json**, creates corresponding Core Data objects and saves them to the persistent store. If you're curious about its UI elements, head over to **Main.storyboard**. There's a table, a navigation bar and a single prototype cell.

- **Team+CoreDataClass & Team+CoreDataProperties**: These files represent a country's team. It's an NSManagedObject subclass with properties for each of its four attributes: teamName, qualifyingZone, imageName and wins. If you're curious about its entity definition, head over to **WorldCup.xcdatamodel**.

- **Assets.xcassets**: The sample project's asset catalog contains a flag image for every country in **seed.json**.

The first three chapters of this book covered the Core Data concepts mentioned above. If "managed object subclass" doesn't ring a bell or if you're unsure what a Core Data stack is supposed to do, you may want to go back and reread the relevant chapters. NSFetchedResultsController will be here when you return.

Otherwise, if you're ready to proceed, you'll begin implementing the World Cup application. You probably already know who won the World Cup last time, but this is your chance to rewrite history for the country of your choice, with just a few taps!

It all begins with a fetch request...

At its core, NSFetchedResultsController is a wrapper around the results of an NSFetchRequest. Right now, the sample project contains static information. You're going to create a fetched results controller to display the list of teams from Core Data in the table view.

Open **ViewController.swift** and add a lazy property to hold your fetched results controller below coreDataStack:

```
lazy var fetchedResultsController:
  NSFetchedResultsController<Team> = {
  // 1
  let fetchRequest: NSFetchRequest<Team> = Team.fetchRequest()

  // 2
  let fetchedResultsController = NSFetchedResultsController(
    fetchRequest: fetchRequest,
    managedObjectContext: coreDataStack.managedContext,
    sectionNameKeyPath: nil,
    cacheName: nil)

  return fetchedResultsController
}()
```

Like NSFetchRequest, NSFetchedResultsController requires a generic type parameter, Team in this case, to specify the type of entity you *expect* to be working with. Let's go step-by-step through the process:

1. The fetched results controller handles the coordination between Core Data and your table view, but it still needs you to provide an NSFetchRequest. Remember the NSFetchRequest class is highly customizable. It can take sort descriptors, predicates, etc.

   In this example, you get your NSFetchRequest directly from the Team class because you want to fetch all Team objects.

2. The initializer method for a fetched results controller takes four parameters: first up, the fetch request you just created.

    The second parameter is an instance of NSManagedObjectContext. Like NSFetchRequest, the fetched results controller class needs a managed object context to execute the fetch. It can't actually fetch anything by itself.

    The other two parameters are optional: sectionNameKeyPath and cacheName. Leave them blank for now; you'll read more about them later in the chapter.

Next, add the following code to the end of viewDidLoad() to actually do the fetching:

```
do {
  try fetchedResultsController.performFetch()
} catch let error as NSError {
  print("Fetching error: \(error), \(error.userInfo)")
}
```

Here you execute the fetch request. If there's an error, you log the error to the console.

But wait a minute... where are your fetched results? While fetching with NSFetchRequest returns an array of results, fetching with NSFetchedResultsController doesn't return anything.

NSFetchedResultsController is both a wrapper around a fetch request and a container for its fetched results. You can get them either with the fetchedObjects property or the object(at:) method.

Next, you'll connect the fetched results controller to the usual table view data source methods. The fetched results determine both the number of sections and the number of rows per section.

With this in mind, reimplement numberOfSections(in:) and tableView(_:numberOfRowsInSection:), as shown below:

```
func numberOfSections(in tableView: UITableView) -> Int {

  return fetchedResultsController.sections?.count ?? 0
}

func tableView(_ tableView: UITableView,
               numberOfRowsInSection section: Int)
               -> Int {

  guard let sectionInfo =
```

```
        fetchedResultsController.sections?[section] else {
          return 0
  }

  return sectionInfo.numberOfObjects
}
```

The number of sections in the table view corresponds to the number of sections in the fetched results controller. You may be wondering how this table view can have more than one section. Aren't you simply fetching and displaying all teams?

That's correct. You will only have one section this time around, but keep in mind that NSFetchedResultsController can split up your data into sections. You'll see an example of this later in the chapter.

Furthermore, the number of rows in each table view section corresponds to the number of objects in each fetched results controller section. You can query information about a fetched results controller section through its sections property.

> **Note**: The sections array contains opaque objects that implement the NSFetchedResultsSectionInfo protocol. This lightweight protocol provides information about a section, such as its title and number of objects.

Implementing tableView(_:cellForRowAt:) would typically be the next step.

A quick look at the method, however, reveals it's already vending TeamCell cells as necessary. What you need to change is the helper method that populates the cell.

Find configure(cell:for:) and replace it with the following:

```
func configure(cell: UITableViewCell,
               for indexPath: IndexPath) {

  guard let cell = cell as? TeamCell else {
      return
  }

  let team = fetchedResultsController.object(at: indexPath)
  cell.teamLabel.text = team.teamName
  cell.scoreLabel.text = "Wins: \(team.wins)"

  if let imageName = team.imageName {
    cell.flagImageView.image = UIImage(named: imageName)
  } else {
```

```
        cell.flagImageView.image = nil
    }
}
```

This method takes in a table view cell and an index path. You use this index path to grab the corresponding Team object from the fetched results controller.

Next, you use the Team object to populate the cell's flag image, team name and score label.

Notice again there's no array variable holding your teams. They're all stored inside the fetched results controller and you access them via object(at:).

It's time to test your creation. Build and run the app. Ready, set and... crash?

```
*** Terminating app due to uncaught exception
'NSInvalidArgumentException', reason: 'An instance of
NSFetchedResultsController requires a fetch request with sort
descriptors'
*** First throw call stack:
(
    0   CoreFoundation                      0x00007fff23b60e3e
__exceptionPreprocess + 350
    1   libobjc.A.dylib                     0x00007fff502f3b20
objc_exception_throw + 48
    2   CoreData                            0x00007fff238a147d -
[NSFetchedResultsController dealloc] + 0
    --- snip! ---
    30  libdyld.dylib                       0x00007fff51175cf5
start + 1
)
libc++abi.dylib: terminating with uncaught exception of type
NSException
```

What happened? NSFetchedResultsController is helping you out here, though it may not feel like it!

If you want to use it to populate a table view and have it know which managed object should appear at which index path, you can't just throw it a basic fetch request.

The key part of the crash log is this:

```
'An instance of NSFetchedResultsController requires a fetch
request with sort descriptors'
```

A regular fetch request doesn't require a sort descriptor.

Its minimum requirement is you set an entity description, and it will fetch all objects of that entity type. `NSFetchedResultsController`, however, requires at least one sort descriptor. Otherwise, how would it know the right order for your table view?

Go back to the `fetchedResultsController` lazy property and add the following lines after `let fetchRequest: NSFetchRequest<Team> = Team.fetchRequest()`:

```
let sort = NSSortDescriptor(key: #keyPath(Team.teamName),
                            ascending: true)
fetchRequest.sortDescriptors = [sort]
```

Adding this sort descriptor will show the teams in alphabetical order from A to Z and fix the earlier crash. Build and run the application.

Success! The full list of World Cup participants is on your device or iOS Simulator. Notice, however, that every country has zero wins and there's no way to increment the score. Some people say soccer is a low-scoring sport, but this is absurd!

Modifying data

Let's fix everyone's zero score and add some code to increment the number of wins. Still in **ViewController.swift**, replace the currently empty implementation of the table view delegate method `tableView(_:didSelectRowAt:)` with the following:

```
func tableView(_ tableView: UITableView,
               didSelectRowAt indexPath: IndexPath) {

  let team = fetchedResultsController.object(at: indexPath)
  team.wins = team.wins + 1
  coreDataStack.saveContext()
}
```

When the user taps a row, you grab the Team corresponding to the selected index path, increment its number of wins and commit the change to Core Data's persistent store.

You might think a *fetched results controller* is only good for fetching results from Core Data, but the Team objects you get back are the same old managed object subclasses. You can update their values and save just as you've always done.

Build and run once again, and tap on the first country on the list (Algeria) three times:

What's going on here? You're tapping away, but the number of wins isn't going up. You're updating Algeria's number of wins in Core Data's underlying persistent store, but you aren't triggering a UI refresh. Go back to Xcode, stop the app, and build and run again.

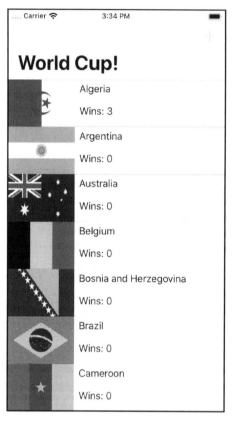

Just as you suspected, re-launching the app from scratch forced a UI refresh, showing Algeria's real score of 3. NSFetchedResultsController has a nice solution to this problem, but for now, let's use the brute force solution.

Add the follow line to the end of tableView(_:didSelectRowAt:):

```
tableView.reloadData()
```

In addition to incrementing a team's number of wins, tapping a cell now reloads the entire table view. This approach is heavy-handed, but it does the job for now. Build and run the app one more time.

Tap as many countries as you want, as many times as you want. Verify that the UI is always up to date.

There you go. You've got a fetched results controller up and running. Excited?

If this were all NSFetchedResultsController could do, you would probably feel a little disappointed. After all, you can accomplish the same thing using an NSFetchRequest and a simple array.

The real magic comes in the remaining sections of this chapter. NSFetchedResultsController earns its keep in the Cocoa Touch frameworks with features such as section handling and change monitoring, which you'll cover next.

Grouping results into sections

There are six qualifying zones in the World Cup: Africa, Asia, Oceania, Europe, South America and North/Central America. The Team entity has a string attribute named `qualifyingZone` storing this information.

In this section, you'll split up the list of countries into their respective qualifying zones. `NSFetchedResultsController` makes this very simple.

Let's see it in action. Go back to the lazy property that instantiates your `NSFetchedResultsController` and make the following change to the fetched results controller's initializer:

```
let fetchedResultsController = NSFetchedResultsController(
  fetchRequest: fetchRequest,
  managedObjectContext: coreDataStack.managedContext,
  sectionNameKeyPath: #keyPath(Team.qualifyingZone),
  cacheName: nil)
```

The difference here is you're passing in a value for the optional `sectionNameKeyPath` parameter. You can use this parameter to specify an attribute the fetched results controller should use to group the results and generate sections.

How exactly are these sections generated? Each unique attribute value becomes a section. `NSFetchedResultsController` then groups its fetched results into these sections. In this case, it will generate sections for each unique value of `qualifyingZone` such as "Africa", "Asia", "Oceania" and so on. This is exactly what you want!

> **Note**: `sectionNameKeyPath` takes a keyPath string. It can take the form of an attribute name such as `qualifyingZone` or `teamName`, or it can drill deep into a Core Data relationship, such as `employee.address.street`. Use the `#keyPath` syntax to defend against typos and stringly typed code.

The fetched results controller will now report the sections and rows to the table view, but the current UI won't look any different. To fix this problem, add the following method to the `UITableViewDataSource` extension:

```
func tableView(_ tableView: UITableView,
               titleForHeaderInSection section: Int)
               -> String? {
  let sectionInfo = fetchedResultsController.sections?[section]
  return sectionInfo?.name
}
```

Implementing this data source method adds section headers to the table view, making it easy to see where one section ends and another one begins. In this case, the section gets its title from the qualifying zone. Like before, this information comes directly from the `NSFetchedResultsSectionInfo` protocol.

Build and run the application. Your app will look something like the following:

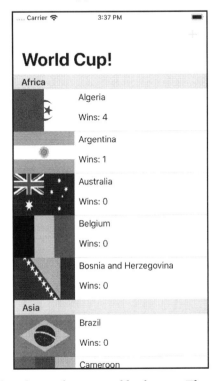

Scroll down the page. There's good news and bad news. The good news is the app accounts for all six sections. Hooray! The bad news is the world is upside down.

Take a closer look at the sections. You'll see Argentina in Africa, Cameroon in Asia and Russia in South America. How did this happen? It's not a problem with the data; you can open **seed.json** and verify each team lists the correct qualifying zone.

Have you figured it out? The list of countries is still shown alphabetically and the fetched results controller is simply splitting up the table into sections as if all teams of the same qualifying zone were grouped together.

Go back to your lazily-instantiated `NSFetchedResultsController` property and make the following change to fix the problem.

Replace the existing code that creates and sets the sort descriptor on the fetch request with the following:

```
let zoneSort = NSSortDescriptor(
  key: #keyPath(Team.qualifyingZone), ascending: true)
let scoreSort = NSSortDescriptor(
  key: #keyPath(Team.wins), ascending: false)
let nameSort = NSSortDescriptor(
  key: #keyPath(Team.teamName), ascending: true)

fetchRequest.sortDescriptors = [zoneSort, scoreSort, nameSort]
```

The problem was the sort descriptor. This is another NSFetchedResultsController "gotcha" to keep in mind. If you want to separate fetched results using a section keyPath, the first sort descriptor's attribute must match the key path's attribute.

The documentation for NSFetchedResultsController makes this point emphatically, and with good reason! You saw what happened when the sort descriptor doesn't match the key path — there's no sense to your data.

Build and run one more time to verify this change fixed the problem:

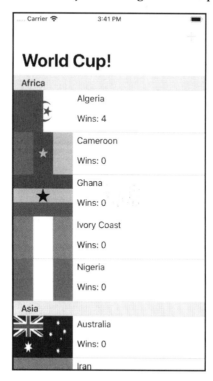

Indeed it did. Changing the sort descriptor restored the geopolitical balance in your sample application. African teams are in Africa, European teams are in Europe and so on.

> **Note**: The only team that may still raise eyebrows is Australia, which appears under Asia's qualifying zone. This is how FIFA categorizes Australia. If you don't like it, you can file a bug report with them!

Notice that within each qualifying zone, teams are sorted by number of wins from highest to lowest, then by name. This is because in the previous code snippet, you added three sort descriptors: first sort by qualifying zone, then by number of wins, then finally by name.

Before moving on, take a moment to think of what you would have needed to do to separate the teams by qualifying zone *without* the fetched results controller. First, you would have had to create a dictionary and iterate over the teams to find unique qualifying zones.

As you traversed the array of teams, you would have had to associate each team with the correct qualifying zone. Once you had the list of teams by zone, you'd then would have had to sort the data.

Of course it's not impossible to do this yourself, but it's tedious. This is what `NSFetchedResultsController` saved you from doing. You can take the rest of the day off and go to the beach or watch some old World Cup matches. Thank you, `NSFetchedResultsController`!

"Cache" the ball

As you can probably imagine, grouping teams into sections is not a cheap operation. There's no way to avoid iterating over every team.

It's not a performance problem in this case, because there are only 32 teams to consider. But imagine what would happen if your data set were much larger. What if your task were to iterate over 3 million census records and separate them by state or province?

"I'd just throw that on a background thread!" might be your first thought. The table view, however, can't populate itself until all sections are available. You might save yourself from blocking the main thread, but you'd still be left looking at a spinner.

There's no denying that this operation is expensive. At a bare minimum, you should only pay the cost once: figure out the section grouping a single time, and reuse your result every time after that.

The authors of NSFetchedResultsController thought about this problem and came up with a solution: caching. You don't have to do much to turn it on.

Head back to your lazily instantiated NSFetchedResultsController and make the following modification to the fetched results controller initialization, adding a value to the cacheName parameter:

```
let fetchedResultsController = NSFetchedResultsController(
  fetchRequest: fetchRequest,
  managedObjectContext: coreDataStack.managedContext,
  sectionNameKeyPath: #keyPath(Team.qualifyingZone),
  cacheName: "worldCup")
```

You specify a cache name to turn on NSFetchedResultsController's on-disk section cache. That's all you need to do! Keep in mind that this section cache is completely separate from Core Data's persistent store, where you persist the teams.

> **Note**: NSFetchedResultsController's section cache is very sensitive to changes in its fetch request. As you can imagine, any changes — such as a different entity description or different sort descriptors — would give you a completely different set of fetched objects, invalidating the cache completely. If you make changes like this, you must delete the existing cache using deleteCache(withName:) or use a different cache name.

Build and run the application a few times. The second launch should be a *little* bit faster than the first. This is not the author's power of suggestion (psst, say "fast" five times in a row); it's NSFetchedResultsController's cache system at work!

On the second launch, NSFetchedResultsController reads directly from your cache. This saves a round trip to Core Data's persistent store, as well as the time needed to compute those sections. Hooray!

You'll learn about measuring performance and seeing if your code changes really did make things faster in Chapter 8, "Measuring and Boosting Performance".

In your own apps, consider using `NSFetchedResultsController`'s cache if you're grouping results into sections and either have a very large data set or are targeting older devices.

Monitoring changes

This chapter has already covered two of the three main benefits of using `NSFetchedResultsController`: sections and caching. The third and last benefit is somewhat of a double-edged sword: it's powerful but also easy to misuse.

Earlier in the chapter, when you implemented the tap to increment the number of wins, you added a line of code to reload the table view to show the updated score. This was a brute force solution, but it worked.

Sure, you could have reloaded only the selected cell by being smart about the `UITableView` API, but that wouldn't have solved the root problem.

Not to get too philosophical, but the root problem is *change*. Something changed in the underlying data and you had to be explicit about reloading the user interface.

Imagine what a second version of the World Cup app would look like. Maybe there's a detail screen for every team where you can change the score.

Maybe the app calls an API endpoint and gets new score information from the web service. It would be your job to refresh the table view for *every code path* that updates the underlying data.

Doing it explicitly is error-prone, not to mention a little boring. Isn't there a better way? Yes, there is. Once again, fetched results controller comes to the rescue.

`NSFetchedResultsController` can listen for changes in its result set and notify its delegate, `NSFetchedResultsControllerDelegate`. You can use this delegate to refresh the table view as needed any time the underlying data changes.

What does it mean a fetched results controller can monitor changes in its "result set"? It means it can monitor changes in all objects, old and new, it *would* have fetched, in addition to objects it has already fetched. This distinction will become clearer later in this section.

Let's see this in practice. Add the following extension to the bottom of the file:

```
// MARK: - NSFetchedResultsControllerDelegate
extension ViewController: NSFetchedResultsControllerDelegate {

}
```

This simply tells the compiler the `ViewController` class will implement some of the fetched results controller's delegate methods.

Next, go back to your lazy `NSFetchedResultsController` property and set the view controller as the fetched results controller's delegate before returning. Add the following line of code after you initialize the fetched results controller:

```
fetchedResultsController.delegate = self
```

That's all you need to start monitoring changes! Of course, the next step is to do something when those change reports come in. You'll do that next.

> **Note**: A fetched results controller can only monitor changes made via the managed object context specified in its initializer. If you create a separate `NSManagedObjectContext` somewhere else in your app and start making changes there, your delegate method won't run until those changes have been saved and merged with the fetched results controller's context.0

Responding to changes

First, remove the `reloadData()` call from `tableView(_:didSelectRowAt:)`. As mentioned before, this was the brute force approach that you're now going to replace.

`NSFetchedResultsControllerDelegate` has four methods that come in varying degrees of granularity. To start out, implement the broadest delegate method, the one that says: "Hey, something just changed!"

Add the following method inside the `NSFetchedResultsControllerDelegate` extension:

```
func controllerDidChangeContent(_ controller:
  NSFetchedResultsController<NSFetchRequestResult>) {
    tableView.reloadData()
}
```

The change may seem small, but implementing this method means that any change whatsoever, no matter the source, will refresh the table view. Build and run the application. Verify that the table view's cells still update correctly by tapping on a few cells:

The score labels update as before, but there's something else happening. When one country has more points than another country in the same qualifying zone, that country will "jump" up a level. This is the fetched results controller noticing a change in the sort order of its fetched results and readjusting the table view's data source accordingly.

When the cells do move around, it's pretty jumpy... almost as if you were completely reloading the table every time something changed.

Next, you'll go from reloading the entire table to refreshing only what needs to change. The fetched results controller delegate can tell you if a specific index path needs to be moved, inserted or deleted due to a change in the fetched results controller's result set.

Replace the contents of the NSFetchedResultsControllerDelegate extension, with the following three delegate methods to see this in action:

```
func controllerWillChangeContent(_ controller:
  NSFetchedResultsController<NSFetchRequestResult>) {
    tableView.beginUpdates()
}

func controller(_ controller:
  NSFetchedResultsController<NSFetchRequestResult>,
  didChange anObject: Any,
  at indexPath: IndexPath?,
  for type: NSFetchedResultsChangeType,
  newIndexPath: IndexPath?) {

  switch type {
  case .insert:
    tableView.insertRows(at: [newIndexPath!], with: .automatic)
  case .delete:
    tableView.deleteRows(at: [indexPath!], with: .automatic)
  case .update:
    let cell = tableView.cellForRow(at: indexPath!) as! TeamCell
    configure(cell: cell, for: indexPath!)
  case .move:
    tableView.deleteRows(at: [indexPath!], with: .automatic)
    tableView.insertRows(at: [newIndexPath!], with: .automatic)
  @unknown default:
    print("Unexpected NSFetchedResultsChangeType")
  }
}

func controllerDidChangeContent(_ controller:
  NSFetchedResultsController<NSFetchRequestResult>) {
    tableView.endUpdates()
}
```

Whew! That's a wall of code. Fortunately, it's mostly boilerplate and easy to understand. Let's briefly go over all three methods you just added or modified.

- **controllerWillChangeContent(_:):** This delegate method notifies you that changes are about to occur. You ready your table view using beginUpdates().

- **controller(_:didChange:at:for:newIndexPath:):** This method is quite a mouthful. And with good reason — it tells you exactly which objects changed, what type of change occurred (insertion, deletion, update or reordering) and what the affected index paths are.

  This middle method is the proverbial glue that synchronizes your table view with Core Data. No matter how much the underlying data changes, your table view will stay true to what's going on in the persistent store.

- **controllerDidChangeContent(_:):** The delegate method you had originally implemented to refresh the UI turned out to be the third of three delegate methods that notify you of changes. Rather than refreshing the entire table view, you just need to call endUpdates() to apply the changes.

> **Note**: What you end up doing with the change notifications depends on your individual app. The implementation you see above is an example Apple provided in the NSFetchedResultsControllerDelegate documentation.

Note the order and nature of the methods ties in very neatly to the "begin updates, make changes, end updates" pattern used to update table views. This is not a coincidence!

Build and run to see your work in action. Right off the bat, each qualifying zone lists teams by the number of wins. Tap on different countries a few times. You'll see the cells animate smoothly to maintain this order.

First:

Then:

For example, in the first screenshot, Switzerland leads Europe with six wins. Tapping on Bosnia & Herzegovina until their score is also six moves the cell on top of Switzerland with a nice animation. This is the fetched results controller delegate in action!

There is one more `NSFetchedResultsControllerDelegate` method to explore in this section. Add it to the extension:

```
func controller(_ controller:
  NSFetchedResultsController<NSFetchRequestResult>,
  didChange sectionInfo: NSFetchedResultsSectionInfo,
  atSectionIndex sectionIndex: Int,
  for type: NSFetchedResultsChangeType) {

  let indexSet = IndexSet(integer: sectionIndex)

  switch type {
  case .insert:
    tableView.insertSections(indexSet, with: .automatic)
  case .delete:
    tableView.deleteSections(indexSet, with: .automatic)
  default: break
```

```
    }
  }
```

This delegate method is similar to `controllerDidChangeContent(_:)` but notifies you of changes to sections rather than to individual objects. Here, you handle the cases where changes in the underlying data trigger the creation or deletion of an entire section.

Take a moment and think about what kind of change would trigger these notifications. Maybe if a new team entered the World Cup from a completely new qualifying zone, the fetched results controller would pick up on the uniqueness of this value and notify its delegate about the new section.

This would never happen in a standard-issue World Cup. Once the 32 qualifying teams are in the system, there's no way to add a new team. Or is there?

Inserting an underdog

For the sake of demonstrating what happens to the table view when there's an insertion in the result set, let's assume there *is* a way to add a new team.

If you were paying close attention, you may have noticed the + bar button item on the top-right. It's been disabled all this time.

Let's implement this now. In **ViewController.swift** add the following method below `viewDidLoad()`:

```
override func motionEnded(_ motion: UIEvent.EventSubtype,
                         with event: UIEvent?) {
  if motion == .motionShake {
    addButton.isEnabled = true
  }
}
```

You override `motionEnded(_:with:)` so shaking the device enables the + bar button item. This will be your secret way in. The `addButton` property held a reference to this bar button item all along!

Next, add the following extension above the extension marked with `// MARK: -` `Internal`:

```
// MARK: - IBActions
extension ViewController {
```

```swift
@IBAction func addTeam(_ sender: Any) {

  let alertController = UIAlertController(
    title: "Secret Team",
    message: "Add a new team",
    preferredStyle: .alert)

  alertController.addTextField { textField in
    textField.placeholder = "Team Name"
  }

  alertController.addTextField { textField in
    textField.placeholder = "Qualifying Zone"
  }

  let saveAction = UIAlertAction(title: "Save",
                                 style: .default) {
    [unowned self] action in

    guard
      let nameTextField = alertController.textFields?.first,
      let zoneTextField = alertController.textFields?.last
      else {
        return
    }

    let team = Team(
      context: self.coreDataStack.managedContext)

    team.teamName = nameTextField.text
    team.qualifyingZone = zoneTextField.text
    team.imageName = "wenderland-flag"
    self.coreDataStack.saveContext()
  }

  alertController.addAction(saveAction)
  alertController.addAction(UIAlertAction(title: "Cancel",
                                          style: .cancel))

  present(alertController, animated: true)
  }
}
```

This is a fairly long but easy-to-understand method. When the user taps the **Add** button, it presents an alert controller prompting the user to enter a new team.

The alert view has two text fields: one for entering a team name and another for entering the qualifying zone. Tapping **Save** commits the change and inserts the new team into Core Data's persistent store.

The action is already connected in the storyboard, so there's nothing more for you to do. Build and run the app one more time.

If you're running on a device, shake it. If you're running on the Simulator, press **Command + Control + Z** to simulate a shake event.

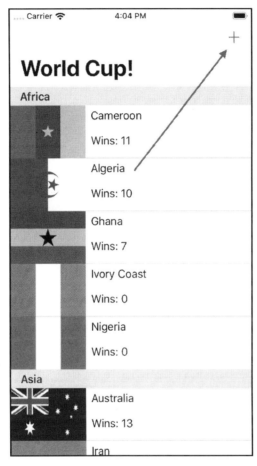

Open sesame! After much negotiation, both parties decided to "shake on it" and the **Add** button is now active!

The World Cup is officially accepting one new team. Scroll down the table to the end of the European qualifying zone and the beginning of the North, Central America & Caribbean qualifying zone. You'll see why in a moment.

Before moving on, take a few seconds to take this in. You're going to change history by adding another team to the World Cup. Are you ready?

Tap the + button on the top right. You'll be greeted by an alert view asking for the new team's details.

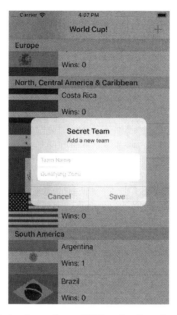

Enter the fictitious (yet thriving) nation of **Wenderland** as the new team. Type **Internets** for qualifying zone and tap **Save**. After a quick animation, your user interface should look like the following:

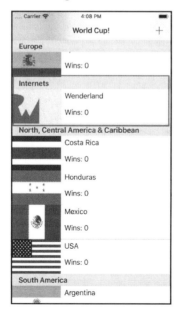

Since "Internets" is a new value for the fetched results controller's `sectionNameKeyPath`, this operation created both a new section and added a new team to the fetched results controller result set.

That handles the data side of things. Additionally, since you implemented the fetched results controller delegate methods appropriately, the table view responded by inserting a new section with one new row.

That's the beauty of `NSFetchedResultsControllerDelegate`. You can set it once and forget it. The underlying data source and your table view will always be synchronized.

As for how the Wenderland flag made it into the app: Hey, we're developers! We need to plan for all kinds of possibilities.

Diffable Data Sources

In iOS 13, Apple introduced a new way to implement table views and collection views: diffable data sources. Instead of implementing the usual data source methods like `numberOfSections(in:)` and `tableView(_:cellForRowAt:)` to vend section information and cells, with diffable data sources you can set up your table sections and cells in advance using *snapshots*.

Along with diffable data sources, there is also a new way of using `NSFetchedResultsController` to monitor changes in a fetch request's result set.

Let's start by removing the existing data source implementation from the sample project. Go ahead and delete the entire `ViewController` extension that conforms to `UITableViewDataSource`. The comment `// MARK: – UITableViewDataSource` marks the beginning.

Then, scroll to the top of **ViewController** and add the following property:

```
var dataSource: UITableViewDiffableDataSource<String, Team>?
```

`UITableViewDiffableDataSource` is generic for two types - one to represent section identifiers, and one to represent item identifiers. Here you're using `String` for sections, and `Team` for items. Both the types must be `Hashable`, because they're used as identifiers.

Add the following new method below `configure(cell:for)`.

```
func setupDataSource()
  -> UITableViewDiffableDataSource<String, Team> {
    return UITableViewDiffableDataSource(tableView: tableView) {
      [unowned self] (tableView, indexPath, team)
      -> UITableViewCell? in

      let cell = tableView.dequeueReusableCell(
        withIdentifier: self.teamCellIdentifier,
        for: indexPath)
      self.configure(cell: cell, for: indexPath)
      return cell
    }
}
```

This method creates your diffable data source. When creating a data source like this, it automatically adds itself as the table view's data source. Notice that you pass in a closure for configuring cells, instead of having a separate method.

Now add this line in `viewDidLoad()`, after `importJSONSeedDataIfNeeded()`

```
dataSource = setupDataSource()
```

In the previous setup, the table view's data source was the view controller. The table view data source will now be the diffable data source object that you set up earlier.

Now find the `NSFetchedResultsControllerDelegate` implementation and delete all four delegate methods that you set up in the previous section:

- `controllerWillChangeContent(_:)`
- `controller(_:didChangeContentWith:)`
- `controllerDidChangeContent(_:)`
- `controller(didChange:atSectionIndex:for:)`

In their place, implement the following delegate method:

```
func controller(
  _ controller:
  NSFetchedResultsController<NSFetchRequestResult>,
  didChangeContentWith
  snapshot: NSDiffableDataSourceSnapshotReference) {

  //1
  var diff = NSDiffableDataSourceSnapshot<String, Team>()
  snapshot.sectionIdentifiers.forEach { section in
```

```
    //2
    diff.appendSections([section as! String])

    //3
    let items =
      snapshot.itemIdentifiersInSection(withIdentifier: section)
      .map { (objectId: Any) -> Team in
        let oid =  objectId as! NSManagedObjectID
        return controller
          .managedObjectContext
          .object(with: oid) as! Team
    }

    diff.appendItems(items, toSection: section as? String)
  }

  //4
  dataSource?.apply(diff)
}
```

The old delegate methods you deleted told you when the changes were about to happen, what the changes were, and when the changes completed.

These delegate calls lined up nicely with methods in UITableView such as beginUpdates() and endUpdates(), which you no longer need to call because you made the switch to diffable data sources.

Instead, the new delegate method gives you a summary of any changes to the fetched result set and passes you a pre-computed snapshot that you can apply to your table view. So much simpler!

Notice that the new delegate method passes you an instance of NSDiffableDataSourceSnapshotReference instead of an instance of the generic type you defined in setupDataSource(), so you need to do some transformations to turn it into something you can apply to your data source:

1. Here you declare an instance of NSDiffableDataSourceSnapshot<String, Team>, which is the type that your table view's data source expects to receive.

2. You take the original snapshot and append each of its sections to the typed snapshot.

3. Take the items from each section in the original snapshot and map it to the corresponding section in the typed snapshot

4. The mapping is now complete and you can safely apply the new snapshot to the data source.

Build and run to see where you are at with the new diffable snapshots:

Great! It seems like most things worked, but there are two problems. First, the console is warning you that the table view is laying out its cells before it's on screen, and the second is that the teams seem to be grouped by qualifying zone but the section headers are gone.

The console warning is happening because things are happening in a different order now. When the view controller was the data source of the table, and you were implementing the old fetched results controller delegate methods, then the table wasn't asking for any information until it was loaded and added to the screen. Now you're using a diffable data source, and the first change happens when you call performFetch() on the results controller, which in turn calls controller(_: didChangeContentWith:), which "adds" in all of the rows from the first fetch. You call performFetch() in viewDidLoad(), which happens before the view is added to the window. Phew!

To fix this, you need to perform the first fetch later on. Remove the do / catch statement from viewDidLoad(), since that's now happening too early in the lifecycle. Implement viewDidAppear(_:), which is called *after* the view is added to the window:

```
override func viewDidAppear(_ animated: Bool) {
  super.viewDidAppear(animated)
  UIView.performWithoutAnimation {
    do {
      try fetchedResultsController.performFetch()
    } catch let error as NSError {
      print("Fetching error: \(error), \(error.userInfo)")
    }
  }
}
```

Build and run, and the console warning will be gone. Now to fix the section headers.

Why have they disappeared? Earlier, when you removed the implementation of UITableViewDataSource, you also removed tableView(_:titleForHeaderInSection:). This method provided the strings to populate the section headers, and without those strings the headers disappeared.

There is no way to turn these headers back on with UITableViewDiffableDataSource so you'll take an alternate route. Find the section that implements UITableViewDelegate methods and implement these two:

```
func tableView(_ tableView: UITableView,
               viewForHeaderInSection section: Int) -> UIView? {

  let sectionInfo = fetchedResultsController.sections?[section]

  let titleLabel = UILabel()
  titleLabel.backgroundColor = .white
  titleLabel.text = sectionInfo?.name

  return titleLabel
}

func tableView(_ tableView: UITableView,
               heightForHeaderInSection section: Int)
  -> CGFloat {
  return 20
}
```

Instead of just returning the title the populate the section headers, these two delegate methods create and return the UILabel to display along with the height of the section header.

Build and run to see if that brought back the missing headers:

The section headers are back, but if you tap on any team cell you'll notice that the number of wins does not go up anymore.

To fix this, find `tableView(_:didSelectRowAt:)` in the `UITableViewDelegate` section and add the following two lines before the end of the method:

```
let cell = tableView.cellForRow(at: indexPath) as! TeamCell
configure(cell: cell, for: indexPath)
```

Doing so updates the cell live so you can see the numbers go up as you tap on each team. Build and run again and confirm that everything works as advertised.

If you got this far, pat yourself on the back. Not only did you re-implement the sample project with diffable data sources, but you also modernized how you monitor changes with the new fetched results controller delegate method. Along the way, you also removed a lot of boilerplate that was previously required.

> **Note**: If you are monitoring changes to manage the state of views that don't support diffable data sources, you should keep in mind there is another `NSFetchedResultsControllerDelegate` method that gives you a summary of all changes to the fetched results in one shot, but uses `CollectionDifference<NSManagedObjectID>` to return the results.

Key points

- **NSFetchedResultsController** abstracts away most of the code needed to synchronize a table view with a Core Data store.

- At its core, `NSFetchedResultsController` is a wrapper around an **NSFetchRequest** and a container for its **fetched results**.

- A fetched results controller requires setting at least **one sort descriptor** on its fetch request. If you forget the sort descriptor, your app will crash.

- You can set a fetched result's controller **sectionNameKeyPath** to specify an attribute to group the results into table view **sections**. Each unique value corresponds to a different table view section.

- Grouping a set of fetched results into sections is an expensive operation. Avoid having to compute sections multiple times by specifying a **cache name** on your fetched results controller.

- A fetched results controller can listen for changes in its result set and notify its **delegate**, `NSFetchedResultsControllerDelegate`, to respond to these changes.

- `NSFetchedResultsControllerDelegate` monitors changes in individual Core Data records (whether they were inserted, deleted or modified) as well as changes to entire sections.

- Diffable data sources make working with fetched results controllers and table views easier.

Where to go from here?

You've seen how powerful and useful NSFetchedResultsController can be, and you've learned how well it works together with a table view. Table views are so common in iOS apps and you've seen first hand how the fetched results controller can save you a lot of time and code!

With some adaptation to the delegate methods, you can also use a fetched results controller to drive a collection view — the main difference being that collection views don't bracket their updates with begin and end calls, so it's necessary to store up the changes and apply them all in a batch at the end.

There are a few things you should bear in mind before using fetched results controllers in other contexts. Be mindful of how you implement the fetched results controller delegate methods. Even the slightest change in the underlying data will fire those change notifications, so avoid performing any expensive operations that you're not comfortable performing over and over.

It's not every day that a single class gets an entire chapter in a book; that honor is reserved for the select few. NSFetchedResultsController is one of them. As you've seen in this chapter, the reason this class exists is to save you time.

NSFetchedResultsController is important for another reason: it fills a gap that iOS developers have faced compared to their macOS developer counterparts. Unlike iOS, macOS has Cocoa bindings, which provide a way to tightly couple a view with its underlying data model. Sound familiar?

If you ever find yourself writing complex logic to compute sections or breaking a sweat trying to get your table view to play nicely with Core Data, think back to this chapter!

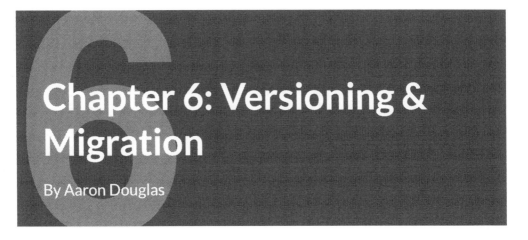

Chapter 6: Versioning & Migration

By Aaron Douglas

You've seen how to design your data model and `NSManagedObject` subclasses in your Core Data apps. During app development, well before the ship date, thorough testing can help iron out the data model. However, changes in app usage, design or features after an app's release will inevitably lead to changes in the data model. What do you do then?

You can't predict the future, but with Core Data, you can migrate toward the future with every new release of your app. The migration process will update data created with a previous version of the data model to match the current data model.

This chapter discusses the many aspects of Core Data migrations by walking you through the evolution of a note-taking app's data model.

You'll start with a simple app with only a single entity in its data model. As you add more features and data to the app, the migrations you do in this chapter will become progressively more complex.

Let the great migration begin!

When to migrate

When is a migration necessary? The easiest answer to this common question is "when you need to make changes to the data model."

However, there are some cases in which you can avoid a migration. If an app is using Core Data merely as an offline cache, when you update the app, you can simply delete and rebuild the data store. This is only possible if the source of truth for your user's data isn't in the data store. In all other cases, you'll need to safeguard your user's data.

That said, any time it's impossible to implement a design change or feature request without changing the data model, you'll need to create a new version of the data model and provide a migration path.

The migration process

When you initialize a Core Data stack, one of the steps involved is adding a store to the persistent store coordinator. When you encounter this step, Core Data does a few things prior to adding the store to the coordinator. First, Core Data analyzes the store's model version. Next, it compares this version to the coordinator's configured data model. If the store's model version and the coordinator's model version don't match, Core Data will perform a migration, when enabled.

> **Note:** If migrations aren't enabled, and the store is incompatible with the model, Core Data will simply not attach the store to the coordinator and specify an error with an appropriate reason code.

To start the migration process, Core Data needs the original data model and the destination model. It uses these two versions to load or create a mapping model for the migration, which it uses to convert data in the original store to data that it can store in the new store. Once Core Data determines the mapping model, the migration process can start in earnest.

Migrations happen in three steps:

1. First, Core Data copies over all the objects from one data store to the next.

2. Next, Core Data connects and relates all the objects according to the relationship mapping.

3. Finally, enforce any data validations in the destination model. Core Data disables destination model validations during the data copy.

You might ask, "If something goes wrong, what happens to the original source data store?" With nearly all types of Core Data migrations, nothing happens to the original store unless the migration completes without error. Only when a migration is successful, will Core Data remove the original data store.

Types of migrations

In my own experience, I've found there are a few more migration variants than the simple distinction between lightweight and heavyweight migrations that Apple calls out. Below, I've provided the more subtle variants of migration names, but these names are not official categories by any means. You'll start with the least complex form of migration and end with the most complex form.

Lightweight migrations

Lightweight migration is Apple's term for the migration with the least amount of work involved on your part. This happens automatically when you use `NSPersistentContainer`, or you have to set some flags when building your own Core Data stack. There are some limitations on how much you can change the data model, but because of the small amount of work required to enable this option, it's the ideal setting.

Manual migrations

Manual migrations involve a little more work on your part. You'll need to specify how to map the old set of data onto the new set, but you get the benefit of a more explicit mapping model file to configure. Setting up a mapping model in Xcode is much like setting up a data model, with similar GUI tools and some automation.

Custom manual migrations

This is level 3 on the migration complexity index. You'll still use a mapping model, but complement that with custom code to specify custom transformation logic on data. Custom entity transformation logic involves creating an `NSEntityMigrationPolicy` subclass and performing custom transformations there.

Fully manual migrations

Fully manual migrations are for those times when even specifying custom transformation logic isn't enough to fully migrate data from one model version to another. Custom version detection logic and custom handling of the migration process are necessary. In this chapter, you'll set up a fully manual migration to update data across non-sequential versions, such as jumping from version 1 to 4.

Throughout this chapter, you'll learn about each of these migration types and when to use them. Let's get started!

Getting started

Included with the resources for this book is a starter project called UnCloudNotes. Find the starter project and open it in Xcode.

Build and run the app in the iPhone simulator. You'll see an empty list of notes:

Tap the plus (+) button in the top-right corner to add a new note. Add a title (there's default text in the note body to make the process faster) and tap Create to save the new note to the data store. Repeat this a few times so you have some sample data to migrate.

Back in Xcode, open the **UnCloudNotesDatamodel.xcdatamodeld** file to show the entity modeling tool in Xcode. The data model is simple — just one entity, a Note, with a few attributes.

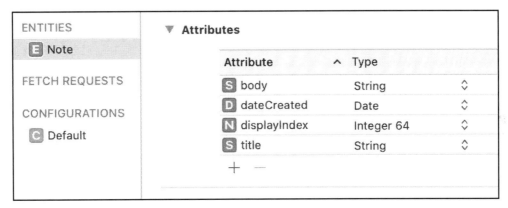

You're going to add a new feature to the app: the ability to attach a photo to a note. The data model doesn't have any place to persist this kind of information, so you'll need to add a place in the data model to hold onto the photo. But you already added a few test notes in the app. How can you change the model without breaking the existing notes?

It's time for your first migration!

A lightweight migration

In Xcode, select the UnCloudNotes data model file if you haven't already. This will show you the Entity Modeler in the main work area. Next, open the Editor menu and select **Add Model Version...**. Name the new version UnCloudNotesDataModel v2 and ensure UnCloudNotesDataModel is selected in the Based on model field. Xcode will now create a copy of the data model.

> **Note:** You can give this file any name you want. The sequential v2, v3, v4, et cetera naming helps you easily tell the versions apart.

This step will create a second version of the data model, but you still need to tell Xcode to use the new version as the current model. If you forget this step, selecting the top level **UnCloudNotesDataModel.xcdatamodeld** file will perform any changes you make to the original model file. You can override this behavior by selecting an individual model version, but it's still a good idea to make sure you don't accidentally modify the original file.

In order to perform any migration, you want to keep the original model file as it is, and make changes to an entirely new model file.

In the `File Inspector` pane on the right, there is a selection menu toward the bottom called Model Version.

Change that selection to match the name of the new data model, `UnCloudNotesDataModel v2`.

Once you've made that change, notice that the little green check mark icon in the project navigator has moved from the previous data model to the v2 data model:

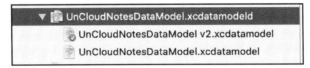

Core Data will try to first connect the persistent store with the ticked model version when setting up the stack. If a store file was found, and it isn't compatible with this model file, a migration will be triggered. The older version is there to support migration. The current model is the one Core Data will ensure is loaded prior to attaching the rest of the stack for your use.

Make sure you have the v2 data model selected and add an **image** attribute to the Note entity. Set the attribute's name to image and the attribute's type to **Transformable**.

Since this attribute is going to contain the actual binary bits of the image, you'll use a custom NSValueTransformer to convert from binary bits to a UIImage and back again. Just such a transformer has been provided for you in ImageTransformer. In the Data Model Inspector on the right of the screen, look for the Value Transformer field, and enter **ImageTransformer**. Next, in the Module field, choose **Current Product Module**.

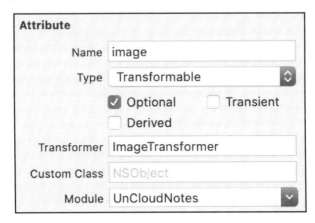

> **Note**: When referencing code from your model files, just like in Xib and Storyboard files, you'll need to specify a **module** (UnCloudNotes or Current Product Module depending on what your drop down provides) to allow the class loader to find the exact code you want to attach.

The new model is now ready for some code! Open **Note.swift** and add the following property below `displayIndex`:

```
@NSManaged var image: UIImage?
```

Build and run the app. You'll see your notes are still magically displayed! It turns out lightweight migrations are enabled by default. This means every time you create a new data model version, and it *can* be auto migrated, it will be. What a time saver!

Inferred mapping models

It just so happens Core Data can infer a mapping model in many cases when you enable the `shouldInferMappingModelAutomatically` flag on the `NSPersistentStoreDescription`. Core Data can automatically look at the differences in two data models and create a mapping model between them.

For entities and attributes that are identical between model versions, this is a straightforward data pass through mapping. For other changes, just follow a few simple rules for Core Data to create a mapping model.

In the new model, changes must fit an obvious migration pattern, such as:

• Deleting entities, attributes or relationships

• Renaming entities, attributes or relationships using the `renamingIdentifier`

• Adding a new, optional attribute

• Adding a new, required attribute with a default value

• Changing an optional attribute to non-optional and specifying a default value

• Changing a non-optional attribute to optional

• Changing the entity hierarchy

- Adding a new parent entity and moving attributes up or down the hierarchy

- Changing a relationship from to-one to to-many

- Changing a relationship from non-ordered to-many to ordered to-many (and vice versa)

> **Note**: Check out Apple's documentation for more information on how Core Data infers a lightweight migration mapping: https://developer.apple.com/documentation/coredata/using_lightweight_migration.

As you see from this list, Core Data can detect, and more importantly, automatically react to, a wide variety of common changes between data models.

As a rule of thumb, all migrations, if necessary, should start as lightweight migrations and only move to more complex mappings when the need arises.

As for the migration from `UnCloudNotes` to `UnCloudNotes v2`, the image property has a default value of nil since it's an optional property. This means Core Data can easily migrate the old data store to a new one, since this change follows item 3 in the list of lightweight migration patterns.

Image attachments

Now the data is migrated, you need to update the UI to allow image attachments to new notes. Luckily, most of this work has been done for you.

Open **Main.storyboard** and find the `Create Note` scene. Underneath, you'll see the `Create Note With Images` scene that includes the interface to attach an image.

The `Create Note` scene is attached to a navigation controller with a root view controller relationship. `Control–drag` from the navigation controller to the `Create Note With Images` scene and select the root view controller relationship segue.

This will disconnect the old `Create Note` scene and connect the new, image-powered one instead.

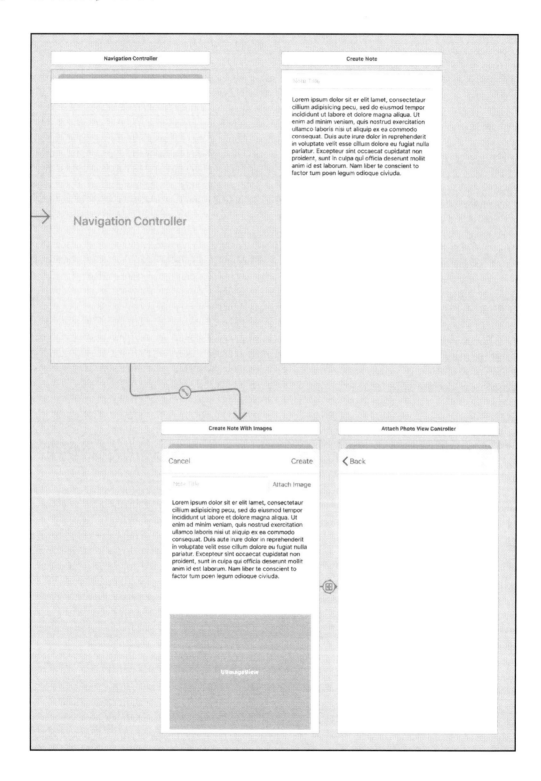

Next, open **AttachPhotoViewController.swift** and add the following method to the
UIImagePickerControllerDelegate extension:

```
func imagePickerController(_ picker: UIImagePickerController,
  didFinishPickingMediaWithInfo info:
  [UIImagePickerController.InfoKey: Any]) {

  guard let note = note else { return }

  note.image =
    info[UIImagePickerController.InfoKey.originalImage] as?
UIImage

  _ = navigationController?.popViewController(animated: true)
}
```

This will populate the new image property of the note once the user selects an image
from the standard image picker.

Next, open **CreateNoteViewController.swift** and replace viewDidAppear(_:) with
the following:

```
override func viewDidAppear(_ animated: Bool) {
  super.viewDidAppear(animated)

  guard let image = note?.image else {
    titleField.becomeFirstResponder()
    return
  }

  attachedPhoto.image = image
  view.endEditing(true)
}
```

This will display the new image if the user has added one to the note.

Next, open **NotesListViewController.swift** and update
tableView(_:cellForRowAt): with the following:

```
override func tableView(_ tableView: UITableView,
                        cellForRowAt indexPath: IndexPath)
                        -> UITableViewCell {

  let note = notes.object(at: indexPath)
  let cell: NoteTableViewCell
  if note.image == nil {
    cell = tableView.dequeueReusableCell(
      withIdentifier: "NoteCell",
      for: indexPath) as! NoteTableViewCell
  } else {
```

```
    cell = tableView.dequeueReusableCell(
      withIdentifier: "NoteCellWithImage",
      for: indexPath) as! NoteImageTableViewCell
  }

  cell.note = note
  return cell
}
```

This will dequeue the correct `UITableViewCell` subclass based on the note having an image present or not. Finally, open **NoteImageTableViewCell.swift** and add the following to `updateNoteInfo(note:)`:

```
noteImage.image = note.image
```

This will update the `UIImageView` inside the `NoteImageTableViewCell` with the image from the note. Build and run, and choose to add a new note:

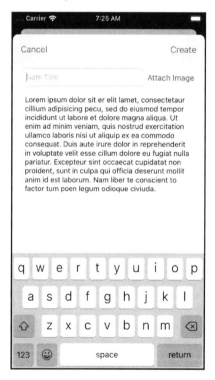

Tap the `Attach Image` button to add an image to the note. Choose an image from your simulated photo library and you'll see it in your new note:

The app uses the standard `UIImagePickerController` to add photos as attachments to notes.

> **Note:** To add your own images to the Simulator's photo album, drag an image file onto the open Simulator window. Thankfully, the iOS Simulator comes with a library of photos ready for your use.

If you're using a device, open **AttachPhotoViewController.swift** and set the `sourceType` attribute on the image picker controller to `.camera` to take photos with the device camera. The existing code uses the photo album, since there is no camera in the Simulator.

Add a couple of sample notes with photos, since in the next section you'll be using the sample data to move forward with a slightly more complex migration.

> **Note**: At this point, you might want to make a copy of the v2 source code into a different folder to come back to later. Or if you're using source control, set a tag here so you can come back to this point. You may also want to save a copy of the data store file and append the name with "v2" for this version of the application as you'll use this later on for more complex migrations.

Congratulations; you've successfully migrated your data and added a new feature based on the migrated data.

A manual migration

The next step in the evolution of this data model is to move from attaching a single image to a note to attaching multiple images. The note entity will stay, and you'll need a new entity for an image. Since a note can have many images, there will be a to-many relationship.

Splitting one entity into two isn't exactly on the list of things lightweight migrations can support. It's time to level up to a custom manual migration!

The first step in every migration is to create a new model version. As before, select the **UnCloudNotesDataModel.xcdatamodeld** file and from the `Editor` menu item, select `Add Model Version....` Name this model `UnCloudNotesDataModel v3` and base it on the v2 data model. Set the new model version as the default model using the option in the `File Inspector Pane`.

Next, you'll add a new entity to the new data model. In the lower-left corner, click the Add Entity button. Rename this entity `Attachment`. Select the entity and in the Data Model Inspector pane, set the Class Name to Attachment, and the Module to `Current Product Module`.

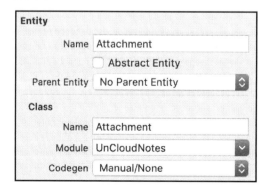

Create two attributes in the `Attachment` entity. Add a non-optional attribute named `image` of type `Transformable`, with the Custom Class transformer field set to `ImageTransformer` and Module field set to `Current Product Module`. This is the same as the image attribute you added to the `Note` entity earlier. Add a second non-optional attribute called `dateCreated` and make it a `Date` type.

Next, add a relationship to the `Note` entity from the `Attachment` entity. Set the relationship name to `note` and its destination to `Note`.

Select the `Note` entity and delete the `image` attribute. Finally, create a to-many relationship from the `Note` entity to the `Attachment` entity. Leave it marked as *Optional*. Name the relationship `attachments`, set the destination to `Attachment` and select the `note` relationship you just created as the inverse.

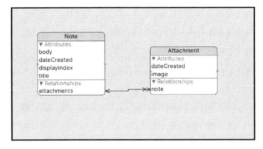

The data model is now ready for migration! While the Core Data model is ready, the code in your app will need some updates to use the changes to the data entities. Remember, you're not working with the `image` property on a `Note` any more, but with multiple `attachments`.

Create a new file called **Attachment.swift** and replace its contents with the following:

```
import Foundation
import UIKit
import CoreData

class Attachment: NSManagedObject {
  @NSManaged var dateCreated: Date
  @NSManaged var image: UIImage?
  @NSManaged var note: Note?
}
```

Next, open **Note.swift** and replace the `image` property with the following:

```
@NSManaged var attachments: Set<Attachment>?
```

The rest of your app still depends on an `image` property, so you'll get a compile error if you try to build the app. Add the following to the `Note` class below `attachments`:

```
var image: UIImage? {
  return latestAttachment?.image
}

var latestAttachment: Attachment? {
  guard let attachments = attachments,
    let startingAttachment = attachments.first else {
      return nil
  }

  return Array(attachments).reduce(startingAttachment) {
    $0.dateCreated.compare($1.dateCreated)
      == .orderedAscending ? $0 : $1
  }
}
```

This implementation uses a computed property, which gets the image from the latest attachment.

If there are several attachments, `latestAttachment` will, as its name suggests, grab the latest one and return it.

Next, open **AttachPhotoViewController.swift**. Update it to create a new `Attachment` object when the user chooses an image. Add the Core Data import to the top of the file:

```
import CoreData
```

Next, replace `imagePickerController(_:didFinishPickingMediaWithInfo:)` with:

```
func imagePickerController(_ picker: UIImagePickerController,
  didFinishPickingMediaWithInfo info:
  [UIImagePickerController.InfoKey: Any]) {

  guard let note = note,
    let context = note.managedObjectContext else {
      return
  }

  let attachment = Attachment(context: context)
  attachment.dateCreated = Date()
  attachment.image =
    info[UIImagePickerController.InfoKey.originalImage] as?
UIImage
  attachment.note = note
```

```
    _ = navigationController?.popViewController(animated: true)
}
```

This implementation creates a new `Attachment` entity adding the image from the `UIImagePickerController` as the `image` property then sets the `note` property of the `Attachment` as the current note.

Mapping models

With lightweight migrations, Core Data can automatically create a mapping model to migrate data from one model version to another when the changes are simple. When the changes aren't as simple, you can manually set up the steps to migrate from one model version to another with a mapping model.

It's important to know that before creating a mapping model, you must complete and finalize your target model.

During the process for creating a new Mapping Model, you'll essentially lock in the source and destination model versions into the Mapping Model file.

This means any changes you make to the actual data model after creating the mapping model will not be seen by the Mapping Model.

Now that you've finished making changes to the v3 data model, you know lightweight migration isn't going to do the job. To create a mapping model, open the File menu in Xcode and select **New ▸ File**.

Navigate to the iOS\Core Data section and select Mapping Model:

Click Next, select the v2 data model as the source model and select the v3 data model as the target model.

Name the new file **UnCloudNotesMappingModel_v2_to_v3**. The file naming convention I typically use is the data model name along with the source version and destination version. As an application collects more and more mapping models over time, this file naming convention makes it easier to distinguish between files and the order in which they have changed over time.

Open **UnCloudNotesMappingModel_v2_to_v3.xcmappingmodel**. Luckily, the mapping model doesn't start completely from scratch; Xcode examines the source and target models and infers as much as it can, so you're starting out with a mapping model that consists of the basics.

Attribute mapping

There are two mappings, one named `NoteToNote` and another simply named `Attachment`. `NoteToNote` describes how to migrate the v2 Note entity to the v3 Note entity.

Select `NoteToNote` and you'll see two sections: **Attribute Mappings** and **Relationship Mappings**.

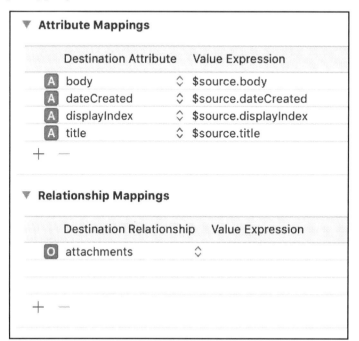

The attributes mappings here are fairly straightforward. Notice the value expressions with the pattern $source. $source is a special token for the mapping model editor, representing a reference to the source instance. Remember, with Core Data, you're not dealing with rows and columns in a database. Instead, you're dealing with objects, their attributes and classes.

In this case, the values for body, dateCreated, displayIndex and title will be transferred directly from the source. Those are the easy cases!

The attachments relationship is new, so Xcode couldn't fill in anything from the source. But, it turns out you'll not be using this particular relationship mapping, so delete this mapping. You'll get to the proper relationship mapping shortly.

Select the Attachment mapping and make sure the Utilities panel on the right is open.

Select the last tab in the Utilities panel to open the Entity Mapping inspector:

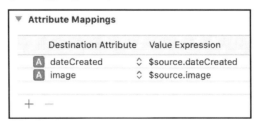

Select Note as the source entity in the drop-down list. Once you select the source entity, Xcode will try to resolve the mappings automatically based on the names of the attributes of the source and destination entities. In this case, Xcode will fill in the dateCreated and image mappings for you:

Xcode will also rename the entity mapping from Attachment to NoteToAttachment. Xcode is being helpful again; it just needs a small nudge from you to specify the source entity. Since the attribute names match, Xcode will fill in the value expressions for you. What does it mean to map data from `Note` entities to `Attachment` entities? Think of this as saying, "For each Note, make an Attachment and copy the image and dateCreated attributes across."

This mapping will create an `Attachment` for every `Note`, but you really only want an `Attachment` if there is an image attached to the note. Make sure the `NoteToAttachment` entity mapping is selected and in the inspector, set the Filter Predicate field to **image != nil**. This will ensure the `Attachment` mapping only occurs when an image is present in the source.

Relationship mapping

The migration is able to copy the images from `Notes` to `Attachments`, but as of yet, there's no relationship linking the `Note` to the `Attachment`. The next step to get that behavior is to add a relationship mapping.

In the `NoteToAttachment` mapping, you'll see a relationship mapping called `note`. Like the relationship mapping you saw in `NoteToNote`, the value expression is empty since Xcode doesn't know how to automatically migrate the relationship.

Select the **NoteToAttachment** mapping. Select the `note` relationship row in the list of relationships so that the Inspector changes to reflect the properties of the relationship mapping. In the Source Fetch field, select **Auto Generate Value Expression**. Enter $source in the Key Path field and select **NoteToNote** from the Mapping Name field.

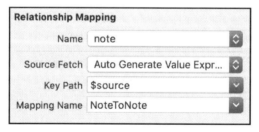

This should generate a value expression that looks like this:

```
FUNCTION($manager,
    "destinationInstancesForEntityMappingNamed:sourceInstances:",
    "NoteToNote", $source)
```

The **FUNCTION** statement resembles the `objc_msgSend` syntax; that is, the first argument is the object instance, the second argument is the selector and any further arguments are passed into that method as parameters.

So, the mapping model is calling a method on the $manager object. The $manager token is a special reference to the NSMigrationManager object handling the migration process.

> **Note**: Using FUNCTION expressions still relies on some knowledge of Objective-C syntax. It might be some time until Apple gets around to porting Core Data 100% to Swift!

Core Data creates the migration manager during the migration. The migration manager keeps track of which source objects are associated with which destination objects. The method destinationInstancesForEntityMappingNamed:sourceInstances: will look up the destination instances for a source object.

The expression on the previous page says "set the note relationship to whatever the $source object for this mapping gets migrated to by the NoteToNote mapping," which in this case will be the Note entity in the new data store. You've completed your custom mapping! You now have a mapping that is configured to split a single entity into two and relate the proper data objects together.

One last thing

Before running this migration, you need to update the Core Data setup code to use this mapping model and not try to infer one on its own.

Open **CoreDataStack.swift** and look for the storeDescription property on to which you set the flags for enabling migrations in the first place. Change the flags to the following:

```
description.shouldMigrateStoreAutomatically = true
description.shouldInferMappingModelAutomatically = false
```

By setting shouldInferMappingModelAutomatically to false, you've ensured that the persistent store coordinator will now use the new mapping model to migrate the store. Yes, that's all the code you need to change; there is no new code!

When Core Data is told not to infer or generate a mapping model, it will look for the mapping model files in the default or main bundle. The mapping model contains the source and destination versions of the model. Core Data will use that information to determine which mapping model, if any, to use to perform a migration. It really is as simple as changing a single option to use the custom mapping model.

Strictly speaking, setting `shouldMigrateStoreAutomatically` to `true` isn't necessary here as `true` is the value by default. But, let's just say, we're going to need this again later.

Build and run the app. You'll notice not a whole lot has changed on the surface! However, if you still see your notes and images as before, the mapping model worked. Core Data has updated the underlying schema of the SQLite store to reflect the changes in the v3 data model.

> **Note**: Again, you might want to make a copy of the v3 source code into a different folder to come back to later. Or if you're using source control, set a tag here so you can come back to this point. Again, you may also want to save a copy of the data store file and append the name with "v3" for this version of the application as you'll use this later on for more complex migrations.

A complex mapping model

The higher-ups have thought of a new feature for `UnCloudNotes`, so you know what that means. It's time to migrate the data model once again! This time, they've decided that supporting only image attachments isn't enough. They want future versions of the app to support videos, audio files or really add any kind of attachment that makes sense.

You make the decision to have a base entity called `Attachment` and a subclass called `ImageAttachment`. This will enable each attachment type to have its own useful information. Images could have attributes for caption, image size, compression level, file size, et cetera. Later, you can add more subclasses for other attachment types.

While new images will grab this information prior to saving, you'll need to extract that information from current images during the migration. You'll need to use either `CoreImage` or the `ImageIO` libraries. These are data transformations that Core Data definitely doesn't support out of the box, which makes a custom manual migration the proper tool for the job.

As usual, the first step in any data migration is to select the data model file in Xcode and select **Editor ▸ Add Model Version...**. This time, create version 4 of the data model called `UnCloudNotesDataModel v4`. Don't forget to set the current version of the data model to v4 in the Xcode Inspector.

Open the v4 data model and add a new entity named `ImageAttachment`. Set the class to `ImageAttachment`, and the module to `Current Product Module`. Make the following changes to `ImageAttachment`:

1. Set the Parent Entity to `Attachment`.

2. Add a required String attribute named `caption`.

3. Add a required Float attribute named `width`.

4. Add a required Float attribute name `height`.

5. Add an optional Transformable attribute named `image`.

6. Set the ValueTransformer to `ImageTransformer`, and set the Module value to `Current Product Module`.

Next, inside the `Attachment` entity:

7. Delete the `image` attribute.

8. If a newRelationship has been automatically created, delete it.

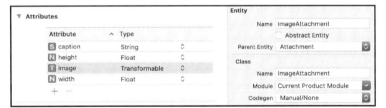

A parent entity is similar to having a parent class, which means `ImageAttachment` will inherit the attributes of `Attachment`. When you set up the managed object subclass later, you'll see this inheritance made explicit in the code.

Before you create the custom code for the mapping model, it'll be easier if you create the `ImageAttachment` source file now. Create a new Swift file called **ImageAttachment** and replace its contents with the following:

```
import UIKit
import CoreData

class ImageAttachment: Attachment {
  @NSManaged var image: UIImage?
  @NSManaged var width: Float
  @NSManaged var height: Float
  @NSManaged var caption: String
}
```

Next, open **Attachment.swift** and delete the image property. Since it's been moved to ImageAttachment, and removed from the Attachment entity in the v4 data model, it should be deleted from the code. That should do it for the new data model. Once you've finished, your version 4 data model should look like this:

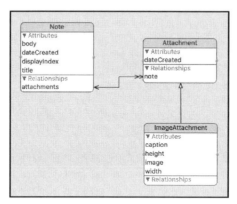

Mapping model

In the Xcode menu, choose **File ▸ New File** and select the **iOS ▸ Core Data ▸ Mapping Model** template. Select version 3 as the source model and version 4 as the target. Name the file **UnCloudNotesMappingModel_v3_to_v4**.

Open the new mapping model in Xcode and you'll see Xcode has again helpfully filled in a few mappings for you.

Starting with the NoteToNote mapping, Xcode has directly copied the source entities from the source store to the target with no conversion or transformation. The default Xcode values for this simple data migration are good to go, as-is!

Select the AttachmentToAttachment mapping. Xcode has also detected some common attributes in the source and target entities and generated mappings. However, you want to convert Attachment entities to ImageAttachment entities. What Xcode has created here will map old Attachment entities to new Attachment entities, which isn't the goal of this migration. Delete this mapping.

Next, select the ImageAttachment mapping. This mapping has no source entity since it's a completely new entity. In the inspector, change the source entity to be Attachment. Now that Xcode knows the source, it will fill in a few of the value expressions for you. Xcode will also rename the mapping to something a little more appropriate, AttachmentToImageAttachment.

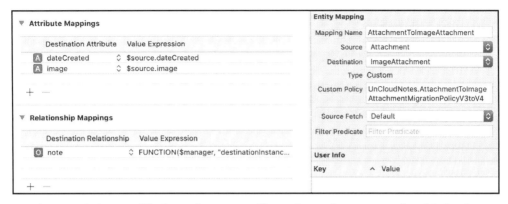

For the remaining, unfilled, attributes, you'll need to write some code. This is where you need image processing and custom code beyond simple FUNCTION expressions! But first, delete those extra mappings, *caption*, *height* and *width*. These values will be computed using a custom migration policy, which happens to be the next section!

Custom migration policies

To move beyond FUNCTION expressions in the mapping model, you can subclass `NSEntityMigrationPolicy` directly. This lets you write Swift code to handle the migration, instance by instance, so you can call on any framework or library available to the rest of your app.

Add a new Swift file to the project called **AttachmentToImageAttachmentMigrationPolicyV3toV4.swift** and replace its contents with the following starter code:

```
import CoreData
import UIKit

let errorDomain = "Migration"

class AttachmentToImageAttachmentMigrationPolicyV3toV4:
  NSEntityMigrationPolicy {

}
```

This naming convention should look familiar to you; it's noting this is a custom migration policy and is for transforming data from `Attachments` in model version 3 to `ImageAttachments` in model version 4.

You'll want to connect this new mapping class to your newly created mapping file before you forget about it. Back in the **v3-to-v4 mapping model file**, select the **AttachmentToImageAttachment** entity mapping. In the `Entity Mapping`

Inspector, fill in the **Custom Policy** field with the fully namespaced class name you just created (including the module):

• **UnCloudNotes.AttachmentToImageAttachmentMigrationPolicyV3toV4**.

When you press Enter to confirm this change, the type above Custom Policy should change to read Custom.

When Core Data runs this migration, it will create an instance of your custom migration policy when it needs to perform a data migration for that specific set of data. That's your chance to run any custom transformation code to extract image information during migration! Now, it's time to add some custom logic to the custom entity mapping policy.

Open **AttachmentToImageAttachmentMigrationPolicyV3toV4.swift** and add the method to perform the migration:

```
override func createDestinationInstances(
  forSource sInstance: NSManagedObject,
  in mapping: NSEntityMapping,
  manager: NSMigrationManager) throws {

  // 1
  let description = NSEntityDescription.entity(
    forEntityName: "ImageAttachment",
    in: manager.destinationContext)
  let newAttachment = ImageAttachment(
    entity: description!,
    insertInto: manager.destinationContext)

  // 2
  func traversePropertyMappings(block:
    (NSPropertyMapping, String) -> ()) throws {
    if let attributeMappings = mapping.attributeMappings {
      for propertyMapping in attributeMappings {
        if let destinationName = propertyMapping.name {
          block(propertyMapping, destinationName)
        } else {
          // 3
          let message =
            "Attribute destination not configured properly"
          let userInfo =
            [NSLocalizedFailureReasonErrorKey: message]
          throw NSError(domain: errorDomain,
                        code: 0, userInfo: userInfo)
        }
      }
    } else {
      let message = "No Attribute Mappings found!"
      let userInfo = [NSLocalizedFailureReasonErrorKey: message]
```

```
        throw NSError(domain: errorDomain,
                      code: 0, userInfo: userInfo)
    }
  }

  // 4
  try traversePropertyMappings {
    propertyMapping, destinationName in
    if let valueExpression = propertyMapping.valueExpression {
      let context: NSMutableDictionary = ["source": sInstance]
      guard let destinationValue =
        valueExpression.expressionValue(with: sInstance,
                                        context: context) else {
          return
      }

      newAttachment.setValue(destinationValue,
                             forKey: destinationName)
    }
  }

  // 5
  if let image = sInstance.value(forKey: "image") as? UIImage {
    newAttachment.setValue(image.size.width, forKey: "width")
    newAttachment.setValue(image.size.height, forKey: "height")
  }

  // 6
  let body =
    sInstance.value(forKeyPath: "note.body") as? NSString ?? ""
  newAttachment.setValue(body.substring(to: 80),
                         forKey: "caption")

  // 7
  manager.associate(sourceInstance: sInstance,
                    withDestinationInstance: newAttachment,
                    for: mapping)
}
```

This method is an override of the default `NSEntityMigrationPolicy` implementation. It's what the migration manager uses to create instances of destination entities. An instance of the source object is the first parameter; when overridden, it's up to the developer to create the destination instance and associate it properly to the migration manager.

Here's what's going on, step by step:

1. First, you create an instance of the new destination object. The migration manager has two Core Data stacks — one to read from the source and one to write to the destination — so you need to be sure to use the destination context here.

Now, you might notice that this section isn't using the new fancy short `ImageAttachment(context: NSManagedObjectContext)` initializer. Well, as it turns out, this migration will simply crash using the new syntax, because it depends on the model having been loaded and finalized, which hasn't happened halfway through a migration.

2. Next, create a `traversePropertyMappings` function that performs the task of iterating over the property mappings if they are present in the migration. This function will control the traversal while the next section will perform the operation required for each property mapping.

3. If, for some reason, the `attributeMappings` property on the `entityMapping` object doesn't return any mappings, this means your mappings file has been specified incorrectly. When this happens, the method will throw an error with some helpful information.

4. Even though it's a custom manual migration, most of the attribute migrations should be performed using the expressions you defined in the mapping model. To do this, use the traversal function from the previous step and apply the value expression to the source instance and set the result to the new destination object.

5. Next, try to get an instance of the image. If it exists, grab its width and height to populate the data in the new object.

6. For the caption, simply grab the note's body text and take the first 80 characters.

7. The migration manager needs to know the connection between the source object, the newly created destination object and the mapping. Failing to call this method at the end of a custom migration will result in missing data in the destination store.

That's it for the custom migration code! Core Data will pick up the mapping model when it detects a v3 data store on launch, and apply it to migrate to the new data model version. Since you added the custom `NSEntityMigrationPolicy` subclass and linked to it in the mapping model, Core Data will call through to your code automatically.

Finally, its time to go back to the main UI code and update the data model usage to take into account the new `ImageAttachment` entity. Open **AttachPhotoViewController.swift** and find `imagePickerController(_:didFinishPickingMediaWithInfo:)`.

Change the line that sets up attachment so it uses `ImageAttachment` instead:

```
let attachment = ImageAttachment(context: context)
```

And while you're here, you should also add a value to the `caption` attribute. The `caption` attribute is a required string value, so if an ImageAttachment is created without a value (ie. a `nil` value), then the save will fail.

Ideally, there would be an extra field from which to enter the value, but add the following line for now:

```
attachment.caption = "New Photo"
```

Next, open **Note.swift** and replace the `image` property with the following:

```
var image: UIImage? {
  let imageAttachment = latestAttachment as? ImageAttachment
  return imageAttachment?.image
}
```

Now that all the code changes have been put in place, you need to update the main data model to use v4 as the main data model.

Select `UnCloudNotesDataModel.xcdatamodeld` in the project navigator. In the Identity pane, under *Model Version* select *UnCloudNotesDataModel v4*.

Build and run the app. The data should migrate properly. Again, your notes will be there, images and all, but you've now future-enabled `UnCloudNotes` to add video, audio and anything else!

Migrating non-sequential versions

Thus far, you've walked through a series of data migrations in order. You've migrated the data from version 1 to 2 to 3 to 4, in sequence. Inevitably, in the real world of App Store launches, a user might skip an update and need to go from version 2 to 4, for example. What happens then?

When Core Data performs a migration, its intention is to perform only a single migration. In this hypothetical scenario, Core Data would look for a mapping model that goes from version 2 to 4; if one didn't exist, Core Data would infer one, if you tell it to. Otherwise the migration will fail, and Core Data will report an error when attempting to attach the store to the persistent store coordinator.

How can you handle this scenario so your requested migration succeeds? You could provide multiple mapping models, but as your app grows, you'd need to provide an inordinate number of these: from v1 to v4, v1 to v3, v2 to v4, et cetera. You would spend more time on mapping models than on the app itself!

The solution is to implement a fully custom migration sequence. You know that the migration from version 2 to 3 works; to go from 2 to 4, it will work well if you manually migrate the store from 2 to 3 and from 3 to 4. This step-by-step migration means you'll prevent Core Data from looking for a direct 2 to 4 or even a 1 to 4 migration.

A self-migrating stack

To begin implementing this solution, you'll want to create a separate `migration manager` class. The responsibility of this class will be to provide a properly migrated Core Data stack, when asked. This class will have a stack property and will return an instance of CoreDataStack, as UnCloudNotes uses throughout, which has run through all the migrations necessary to be useful for the app.

First, create a new Swift file called `DataMigrationManager`. Open the file and replace its contents with the following:

```swift
import Foundation
import CoreData

class DataMigrationManager {
  let enableMigrations: Bool
  let modelName: String
  let storeName: String = "UnCloudNotesDataModel"
  var stack: CoreDataStack

  init(modelNamed: String, enableMigrations: Bool = false) {
    self.modelName = modelNamed
    self.enableMigrations = enableMigrations
  }
}
```

You'll notice that we're going to start this off looking like the current CoreDataStack initializer. That is intended to make this next step a little easier to understand.

Next, open **NotesListViewController.swift** and replace the stack lazy initialization code, as shown below:

```
fileprivate lazy var stack: CoreDataStack =
  CoreDataStack(modelName: "UnCloudNotesDataModel")
```

With:

```
fileprivate lazy var stack: CoreDataStack = {
  let manager = DataMigrationManager(
    modelNamed: "UnCloudNotesDataModel",
    enableMigrations: true)
  return manager.stack
}()
```

You'll use the lazy attribute to guarantee the stack is only initialized once. Second, initialization is actually handled by the DataMigrationManager, so the stack used will be the one returned from the migration manager. As mentioned, the signature of the new DataMigrationManager initializer is similar to the CoreDataStack. That's because you've got a large bit of migration code coming up, and its a good idea to separate the responsibility of migration from the responsibility of saving data.

> **Note:** The project won't build just yet as you've yet to initialize a value for the stack property in the DataMigrationManager. Rest assured, that's coming up soon.

Now to the harder part: How do you figure out if the store needs migrations? And if it does, how do you figure out where to start? In order to do a fully custom migration, you're going to need a little bit of support. First, finding out whether models match or not is not obvious. You'll also need a way to check a persistent store file for compatibility with a model. Let's get started with all the support functions first!

At the bottom of **DataMigrationManager.swift**, add an extension on NSManagedObjectModel:

```
extension NSManagedObjectModel {

  private class func modelURLs(
    in modelFolder: String) -> [URL] {

    return Bundle.main
      .urls(forResourcesWithExtension: "mom",
        subdirectory: "\(modelFolder).momd") ?? []
  }
```

```
class func modelVersionsFor(
  modelNamed modelName: String) -> [NSManagedObjectModel] {

  return modelURLs(in: modelName)
    .compactMap(NSManagedObjectModel.init)
}

class func uncloudNotesModel(
  named modelName: String) -> NSManagedObjectModel {

  let model = modelURLs(in: "UnCloudNotesDataModel")
    .filter { $0.lastPathComponent == "\(modelName).mom" }
    .first
    .flatMap(NSManagedObjectModel.init)
  return model ?? NSManagedObjectModel()
}
}
```

The first method returns all model versions for a given name. The second method returns a specific instance of NSManagedObjectModel named UnCloudNotesDataModel. Usually, Core Data will give you the most recent data model version, but this method will let you dig inside for a specific version.

> **Note**: When Xcode compiles your app into its app bundle, it will also compile your data models. The app bundle will have at its root a .momd folder that contains .mom files. **MOM**, or Managed Object Model, files are the compiled versions of .xcdatamodel files. You'll have a .mom for each data model version.

To use this method, add the following method inside the NSManagedObjectModel class extension:

```
class var version1: NSManagedObjectModel {
  return uncloudNotesModel(named: "UnCloudNotesDataModel")
}
```

This method returns the first version of the data model. That takes care of getting the model, but what about checking the version of a model? Add the following property to the class extension:

```
var isVersion1: Bool {
  return self == type(of: self).version1
}
```

The comparison operator for NSManagedObjectModel isn't very helpful for the purpose of properly checking model equality. To get the == comparison to work on

two NSManagedObjectModel objects, add the following operator function to the file.
You'll need to add this outside of the class extension, right in the global scope:

```
func == (firstModel: NSManagedObjectModel,
         otherModel: NSManagedObjectModel) -> Bool {
  return firstModel.entitiesByName == otherModel.entitiesByName
}
```

The idea here is simple: two NSManagedObjectModel objects are identical if they
have the same collection of entities, with the same version hashes.

Now that everything is set up, you can repeat the version and isVersion pattern for
the next 3 versions. Go ahead and add the following methods for versions 2 to 4 to
the class extension:

```
class var version2: NSManagedObjectModel {
  return uncloudNotesModel(named: "UnCloudNotesDataModel v2")
}

var isVersion2: Bool {
  return self == type(of: self).version2
}

class var version3: NSManagedObjectModel {
  return uncloudNotesModel(named: "UnCloudNotesDataModel v3")
}

var isVersion3: Bool {
  return self == type(of: self).version3
}

class var version4: NSManagedObjectModel {
  return uncloudNotesModel(named: "UnCloudNotesDataModel v4")
}

var isVersion4: Bool {
  return self == type(of: self).version4
}
```

Now that you have a way to compare model versions, you'll need a way to check that
a particular persistent store is compatible with a model version. Add these two
helper methods to the DataMigrationManager class:

```
private func store(at storeURL: URL,
    isCompatibleWithModel model: NSManagedObjectModel) -> Bool {

  let storeMetadata = metadataForStoreAtURL(storeURL: storeURL)

  return model.isConfiguration(
```

```
      withName: nil,
      compatibleWithStoreMetadata:storeMetadata)
}

private func metadataForStoreAtURL(storeURL: URL)
    -> [String: Any] {

  let metadata: [String: Any]
  do {
    metadata = try NSPersistentStoreCoordinator
    .metadataForPersistentStore(ofType: NSSQLiteStoreType,
                                at: storeURL, options: nil)
  } catch {
    metadata = [:]
    print("Error retrieving metadata for store at URL:
      \(storeURL): \(error)")
  }
  return metadata
}
```

The first method is a simple convenience wrapper to determine whether the
persistent store is compatible with a given model. The second method helps by safely
retrieving the metadata for the store.

Next, add the following computed properties to the `DataMigrationManager` class:

```
private var applicationSupportURL: URL {
  let path = NSSearchPathForDirectoriesInDomains(
      .applicationSupportDirectory,
      .userDomainMask, true)
      .first
  return URL(fileURLWithPath: path!)
}

private lazy var storeURL: URL = {
  let storeFileName = "\(self.storeName).sqlite"
  return URL(fileURLWithPath: storeFileName,
              relativeTo: self.applicationSupportURL)
}()

private var storeModel: NSManagedObjectModel? {
  return
    NSManagedObjectModel.modelVersionsFor(modelNamed: modelName)
    .filter {
        self.store(at: storeURL, isCompatibleWithModel: $0)
    }.first
}
```

These properties allow you to access the current store URL and model. As it turns
out, there is no method in the CoreData API to ask a store for its model version.
Instead, the easiest solution is brute force. Since you've already created helper

methods to check if a store is compatible with a particular model, you'll simply need to iterate through all the available models until you find one that works with the store.

Next, you need your migration manager to remember the current model version. To do this, you'll first create a general use method for getting models from a bundle, then you'll simply use that general purpose method to look up the model.

First, add the following method to the `NSManagedObjectModel` class extension:

```
class func model(named modelName: String,
    in bundle: Bundle = .main) -> NSManagedObjectModel {

  return
    bundle
    .url(forResource: modelName, withExtension: "momd")
    .flatMap(NSManagedObjectModel.init)
      ?? NSManagedObjectModel()
}
```

This handy method is used to initialize a managed objet model using the top level folder. Core Data will look for the current model version automatically and load that model into an `NSManagedObjectModel` for use. It's important to note that this method will only work with with Core Data models that have been versioned.

Next, add a property to the `DataMigrationManager` class, as follows:

```
private lazy var currentModel: NSManagedObjectModel =
    .model(named: self.modelName)
```

The `currentModel` property is lazy, so it loads only once since it should return the same thing every time. The .model is the shorthand way of calling the just-added-function that will look up the model from the top level momd folder.

Of course, if the model you have isn't the current model, that's the time to run the migration! Add the following starter method to the `DataMigrationManager` class (which you'll fill in later):

```
func performMigration() {
}
```

Next, replace the stack property definition you added earlier with the following:

```
var stack: CoreDataStack {
  guard enableMigrations,
      !store(at: storeURL,
        isCompatibleWithModel: currentModel)
```

```
  else { return CoreDataStack(modelName: modelName) }

  performMigration()
  return CoreDataStack(modelName: modelName)
}
```

In the end, the computed property will return a CoreDataStack instance. If the migration flag is set, then check if the store specified in the initialization is compatible with what Core Data determines to be the current version of the data model. If the store can't be loaded with the current model, it needs to be migrated. Otherwise, you can use a stack object with whatever version the model is currently set.

You now have a self-migrating Core Data stack that can always be guaranteed to be up to date with the latest model version! Build the project to make sure everything compiles. The next step is to add the custom migration logic.

The self-migrating stack

Now it's time to start building out the migration logic. Add the following method to the DataMigrationManager class:

```
private func migrateStoreAt(URL storeURL: URL,
  fromModel from: NSManagedObjectModel,
  toModel to: NSManagedObjectModel,
  mappingModel: NSMappingModel? = nil) {

  // 1
  let migrationManager =
    NSMigrationManager(sourceModel: from, destinationModel: to)

  // 2
  var migrationMappingModel: NSMappingModel
  if let mappingModel = mappingModel {
    migrationMappingModel = mappingModel
  } else {
    migrationMappingModel = try! NSMappingModel
    .inferredMappingModel(
        forSourceModel: from, destinationModel: to)
  }

  // 3
  let targetURL = storeURL.deletingLastPathComponent()
  let destinationName = storeURL.lastPathComponent + "~1"
  let destinationURL = targetURL
    .appendingPathComponent(destinationName)

  print("From Model: \(from.entityVersionHashesByName)")
```

```swift
print("To Model: \(to.entityVersionHashesByName)")
print("Migrating store \(storeURL) to \(destinationURL)")
print("Mapping model: \(String(describing: mappingModel))")

// 4
let success: Bool
do {
  try migrationManager.migrateStore(from: storeURL,
          sourceType: NSSQLiteStoreType,
          options: nil,
          with: migrationMappingModel,
          toDestinationURL: destinationURL,
          destinationType: NSSQLiteStoreType,
          destinationOptions: nil)
  success = true
} catch {
  success = false
  print("Migration failed: \(error)")
}

// 5
if success {
  print("Migration Completed Successfully")

  let fileManager = FileManager.default
  do {
      try fileManager.removeItem(at: storeURL)
      try fileManager.moveItem(at: destinationURL,
                                to: storeURL)
  } catch {
    print("Error migrating \(error)")
  }
}
}
```

This method does all the heavy lifting. If you need to do a lightweight migration, you can pass `nil` or simply skip the final parameter.

Here's what's going on, step by step:

1. First, you create an instance of the migration manager.

2. If a mapping model was passed in to the method, use that. Otherwise, create an inferred mapping model.

3. Since migrations will create a second data store and migrate data, instance-by-instance, from the original to the new file, the destination URL must be a different file. Now, the example code in this section will create a destinationURL that is the same folder as the original and a file concatenated with "~1". The destination URL can be in a temp folder or anywhere your app has access to write files.

4. Here's where you put the migration manager to work! You've already set it up with the source and destination models, so you simply need to add the mapping model and the two URLs to the mix.

5. Given the result, you can print a success or error message to the console. In the success case, you perform a bit of cleanup, too. In this case, it's enough to remove the old store and replace it with the new store.

Now it's simply a matter of calling that method with the right parameters. Remember your empty implementation of performMigration? It's time to fill that in.

Add the following lines to that method:

```
if !currentModel.isVersion4 {
  fatalError("Can only handle migrations to version 4!")
}
```

This code will only check that the current model is the most recent version of the model. This code bails out and kills the app if the current model is anything other than version 4. This is a little extreme — in your own apps, you might want to continue the migration anyway — but doing it this way will definitely remind you to think about migrations if you ever add another data model version to your app! Thankfully, even though this is the first check in the performMigration method, it should never be run as the next section stops after the last available migration has been applied.

The performMigration method can be improved to handle all known model versions. To do this, add the following below the previously added if-statement:

```
if let storeModel = self.storeModel {
  if storeModel.isVersion1 {
    let destinationModel = NSManagedObjectModel.version2

    migrateStoreAt(URL: storeURL,
             fromModel: storeModel,
               toModel: destinationModel)

    performMigration()
  } else if storeModel.isVersion2 {
```

```
        let destinationModel = NSManagedObjectModel.version3
        let mappingModel = NSMappingModel(from: nil,
                              forSourceModel: storeModel,
                           destinationModel: destinationModel)

        migrateStoreAt(URL: storeURL,
                 fromModel: storeModel,
                   toModel: destinationModel,
              mappingModel: mappingModel)

        performMigration()
      } else if storeModel.isVersion3 {
        let destinationModel = NSManagedObjectModel.version4
        let mappingModel = NSMappingModel(from: nil,
                              forSourceModel: storeModel,
                           destinationModel: destinationModel)

        migrateStoreAt(URL: storeURL,
                 fromModel: storeModel,
                   toModel: destinationModel,
              mappingModel: mappingModel)
      }
    }
```

The steps are similar, no matter which version you start from:

- Lightweight migrations use simple flags to 1) enable migrations, and 2) infer the mapping model. Since the `migrateStoreAt` method will infer a mapping model if one is missing, you've successfully replaced that functionality. By running `performMigration`, you've already enabled migrations.

- Set the destination model to the correct model version. Remember, you're only going "up" one version at a time, so from 1 to 2 and from 2 to 3.

- For version 2 and above, also load the mapping model.

- Finally, call `migrateStoreAt(URL:fromModel:toModel:mappingModel:)`, which you wrote at the start of this section.

What's nice about this solution is that the `DataMigrationManager` class, despite all the comparison support helper functions, is essentially using the mapping models and code that was already defined for each migration.

This solution is manually applying each migration in sequence rather than letting Core Data try to do things automatically.

Note: If you're starting from version 1 or 2, there's a recursive call to performMigration() at the end. This will trigger another run to continue the sequence; once you're at version 3 and run the migration to get to version 4. You will continue adding to this method as you add more data model versions to continue the automatic sequence of migrations.

Testing sequential migrations

Testing this type of migration can be a little complicated, since you need to go back in time and run previous versions of the app to generate data to migrate. If you saved copies of the app project along the way, great!

Otherwise, you'll find previous versions of the project in the resources bundled with the book.

First, make sure you make a copy of the project as it is right now — that's the final project!

Here are the general steps you'll need to take to test each migration:

1. Delete the app from the Simulator to clear out the data store.

2. Open version 2 of the app (so you can at least see some pictures!), and build and run.

3. Create some test notes.

4. Quit the app from Xcode and close the project.

5. Open the final version of the app, and build and run.

At this point, you should see some console output with the migration status. Note the migration will happen prior to the app presenting onscreen.

You now have an app that will successfully migrate between any combinations of old data versions to the latest version.

Key points

- A migration is necessary when you need to make changes to the data model.

- Use the simplest migration method possible.

- Lightweight migration is Apple's term for the migration with the least amount of work involved on your part.

- Heavyweight migrations, as described by Apple, can incorporate several different types of custom migration.

- Custom migrations let you create a mapping model to direct Core Data to make more complex changes that lightweight can't do automatically.

- Once a mapping model has been created, do not change the target model.

- Custom manual migrations go one step further from a mapping model and let you change the model from code.

- Fully manual migrations let your app migrate sequentially from one version to the next preventing issues if a user skips updating their device to a version in between.

- Migration testing is tricky because it is dependent on the data from the source store. Make sure to test several scenarios before releasing your app to the App Store.

Chapter 7: Unit Testing

By Aaron Douglas

Unit testing is the process of breaking down a project into small, testable pieces, or *units*, of software. Rather than test that "the app creates a new record when you tap the button" scenario, you might break this down into testing smaller actions, such as the button touch-up event, creating the entity, and testing whether the save succeeded.

In this chapter, you'll learn how to use the **XCTest** framework in Xcode to test your Core Data apps. Unit testing Core Data apps isn't as straightforward as it could be, because most of the tests will depend on a valid Core Data stack. You might not want a mess of test data from the unit tests to interfere with your own manual testing done in the simulator or on a device, so you'll learn how to keep the test data separate.

Why should you care about unit testing your apps? There are lots of reasons:

- You can shake out the architecture and behavior of your app at a very early stage. You can test much of the app's functionality without needing to worry about the UI.

- You gain the confidence to add features or refactor your project without worrying about breaking things. If you have existing tests that pass, you can be confident the tests will fail if you break something later, so you'll know about the problem immediately.

- You can keep your team of multiple developers from falling over each other as each developer can make and test their changes independently of others.

- You can save time in testing. Instead of tapping through three different screens and entering test data in the fields, you can run a small test for any part of your app's code instead of manually working through the UI.

You'll get a good introduction to XCTest in this chapter, but you should have a basic understanding of it already to get the most from this chapter.

For more information, check out Apple's documentation (https://developer.apple.com/documentation/xctest), our iOS Unit Testing and UI Testing Tutorial (https://www.raywenderlich.com/709-ios-unit-testing-and-ui-testing-tutorial), or our book *iOS 9 by Tutorials*, which includes a chapter on Testing and XCTest.

Getting started

The sample project you'll work with in this chapter, **CampgroundManager**, is a reservation system to track campground sites, the amenities for each site and the campers themselves.

The app is a work in progress. The basic concept: a small campground could use this app to manage their campsites and reservations, including the schedule and payments. The user interface is extremely basic; it's functional but doesn't provide much value. That's OK — in this tutorial, you're never going to build and run the app!

The business logic for the app has been broken down into small pieces. You're going to write unit tests to help with the design. As you develop the unit tests and flesh out the business logic, it'll be easy to see what work remains for the user interface.

The business logic is split into three distinct classes arranged by subject. There's one for campsites, one for campers and one for reservations. All classes have the suffix **Service**, and your tests will focus on these service classes.

Access control

By default, classes in Swift have the "internal" access level. That means you can only access them from within their own modules. Since the app and the tests are in separate targets and separate modules, you normally wouldn't be able to access the classes from the app in your tests.

There are three ways around this issue:

1. You can mark classes and methods in your app as `public` to make them visible from the tests (or open to allow subclassing).

2. You can add classes to the test target in the File Inspector so they will be compiled in, and accessible from, the tests.

3. You can add the Swift keyword `@testable` in front of any import in your unit test to gain access to everything imported in the class.

In the CampgroundManager sample project, the necessary classes and methods in the app target are already marked as `public` or open. That means you'll just need to `import CampgroundManager` from the tests and you'll be able to access whatever you need.

> **Note**: Using `@testable` would be the easiest approach, but its existence in the language is somewhat debatable. In theory, only public methods should be unit tested; anything not `public` isn't testable because there isn't a public interface or contract. Using `@testable` is definitely more acceptable than just blindly adding `public` to all of your classes and functions.

Core Data stack for testing

Since you'll be testing the Core Data parts of the app, the first order of business is getting the Core Data stack set up for testing.

Good unit tests follow the acronym **FIRST**:

- **F**ast: If your tests take too long to run, you won't bother running them.

- **I**solated: Any test should function properly when run on its own or before or after any other test.

- **R**epeatable: You should get the same results every time you run the test against the same codebase.

- **S**elf-verifying: The test itself should report success or failure; you shouldn't have to check the contents of a file or a console log.

- **T**imely: There's some benefit to writing the tests after you've already written the code, particularly if you're writing a new test to cover a new bug. Ideally, though, the tests come first to act as a specification for the functionality you're developing.

When unit tests are executed, the application is started and the test run within the environment of the running app. In practice this can cause problems if the state of the app is being affected by tests running and vice versa. CampgroundManager has been set up to allow the unit test execution to override the AppDelegate. This prevents the app from interfering with the unit tests. Check out `main.swift` and `TestingAppDelegate.swift` for more details.

CampgroundManager uses Core Data to store data in a database file on disk. That doesn't sound very **I**solated, since the data from one test may be written out to the database and could affect other tests. It doesn't sound very **R**epeatable, either, since data will build up in the database file each time you run a test. You could manually delete and recreate the database file before running each test, but that wouldn't be very **F**ast.

The solution is a modified Core Data stack that uses an **in-memory store** instead of an SQLite-backed store. This will be fast and provide a clean slate every time.

The `CoreDataStack` you've been using in most of this book can support multiple contexts, including a background root/parent context to which `NSPersistentStoreCoordinator` is connected. When you use `CoreDataStack` for a test, you want it to access the in-memory store instead of the SQLite database.

Create a new class that subclasses `CoreDataStack` so you can change the store.

1. Right-click **Services** under the **CampgroundManagerTests** group and click **New File**.

2. Select **Swift File** under **iOS ▸ Source**. Click **Next**.

3. Name the file **TestCoreDataStack.swift**. Make sure only the **CampgroundManagerTests** target is selected.

4. Click **Create**.

5. Select **Don't Create** if prompted to add an Objective-C bridging header.

Replace the contents of the file with the following:

```swift
import CampgroundManager
import Foundation
import CoreData

class TestCoreDataStack: CoreDataStack {
  override init() {
    super.init()

    let persistentStoreDescription =
      NSPersistentStoreDescription()
    persistentStoreDescription.type = NSInMemoryStoreType

    let container = NSPersistentContainer(
      name: CoreDataStack.modelName,
      managedObjectModel: CoreDataStack.model)
    container.persistentStoreDescriptions =
      [persistentStoreDescription]

    container.loadPersistentStores { (_, error) in
      if let error = error as NSError? {
        fatalError(
          "Unresolved error \(error), \(error.userInfo)")
      }
    }

    self.storeContainer = container
  }
}
```

This class subclasses `CoreDataStack` and only overrides the default value of a single property: `storeContainer`. Since you're overriding the value in `init()`, the persistent container from `CoreDataStack` isn't used — or even instantiated. The persistent container in `TestCoreDataStack` uses an in-memory store only. An in-memory store is never persisted to disk, which means you can instantiate the stack and write as much data you want in the test. When the test ends — *poof* — the in-memory store clears out automatically. With the stack in place, it's time to create your first test!

> **Note**: There are fundamental differences between how a SQLite store and an in-memory store operate under the covers. You may find your app's specific use cases elicit quirks/bugs specific to SQLite. If your testing situation requires a SQLite store, create a test persistent store using SQLite and provide a different filename than what is used in production. Your `tearDown()` method would then close the test store and delete the file with every test.

Your first test

Unit tests work best when you design your app as a collection of small modules. Instead of throwing all of your business logic into one huge view controller, you create a class (or classes) to encapsulate that logic.

In most cases, you'll probably be adding unit tests to a partially-complete application. In the case of CampgroundManager, the `CamperService`, `CampSiteService` and `ReservationService` classes have already been created, but they aren't yet feature-complete. You'll test the simplest class, `CamperService`, first.

Begin by creating a new test class:

1. Right-click the **Services** group under the **CampgroundManagerTests** group and click **New File**.

2. Select **iOS ▸ Source▸ Unit Test Case Class**. Click **Next**.

3. Name the class **CamperServiceTests**; subclass of **XCTestCase** should already be selected. Choose **Swift** for the language, then click **Next**.

4. Make sure the **CampgroundManagerTests** target checkbox is the only target selected. Click **Create**.

In **CamperServiceTests.swift**, import the app and Core Data frameworks into the test case, along with the other existing `import` statements:

```
import CampgroundManager
import CoreData
```

Next, add the following two properties to the class:

```
// MARK: Properties
var camperService: CamperService!
var coreDataStack: CoreDataStack!
```

These properties will hold references to the `CamperService` instance under test, and to the Core Data stack. The properties are implicitly unwrapped optionals, since they'll be initialized in `setUp` rather than in `init`.

Next, replace the implementation of `setUp` with the following:

```
override func setUp() {
  super.setUp()

  coreDataStack = TestCoreDataStack()
  camperService = CamperService(
    managedObjectContext: coreDataStack.mainContext,
    coreDataStack: coreDataStack)
}
```

`setUp` is called before each test runs. This is your chance to create any resources required by all unit tests in the class. In this case, you initialize the `camperService` and `coreDataStack` properties.

It's wise to reset your data after every test - your tests are **I**solated and **R**epeatable, remember? Using the in-memory store and creating a new context in `setUp` accomplishes this reset for you.

Notice that the `CoreDataStack` instance is actually a `TestCoreDataStack` instance. The `CamperService` initialization method takes the context it needs along with an instance of `CoreDataStack`, since the context save methods are part of that class. You can also use `setUp()` to insert standard test data into the context for use later.

Next, replace `tearDown` with the following implementation:

```
override func tearDown() {
  super.tearDown()

  camperService = nil
  coreDataStack = nil
}
```

`tearDown` is the opposite of `setUp`, and is called after each test executes. Here, the method will simply make all the properties `nil`, resetting `CoreDataStack` after every test.

There's only a single method on `CamperService` at this point:
`addCamper(_:phonenumber:)`. Still in **CamperServiceTests.swift**, create a new
method to test `addCamper`:

```
func testAddCamper() {
  let camper = camperService.addCamper("Bacon Lover",
    phoneNumber: "910-543-9000")

  XCTAssertNotNil(camper, "Camper should not be nil")
  XCTAssertTrue(camper?.fullName == "Bacon Lover")
  XCTAssertTrue(camper?.phoneNumber == "910-543-9000")
}
```

You create a camper with certain properties, then check to confirm a camper exists
with the properties you expect.

Remove the `testExample` and `testPerformanceExample` methods from the class.

It's a simple test, but it ensures if any logic inside of `addCamper` is modified, the basic
operation doesn't change. For example, if you add some new data validation logic to
prevent bacon-loving people from reserving campgrounds, `addCamper` might return
`nil`. This test would then fail, alerting you that either you made a mistake in the
validation or the test needs to be updated.

> **Note**: To round out this test case in a real development context, you'd want to
> write unit tests for strange scenarios such as `nil` parameters, empty
> parameters, or duplicate camper namess.

Run the unit tests by clicking on the **Product** menu, then selecting **Test** (or type
Command+U). You should see a green checkmark in Xcode.

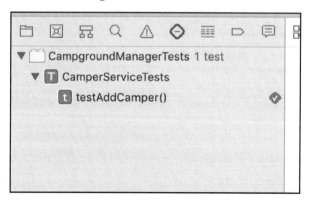

There's your first test! This type of testing is useful for leveraging your data models and checking the attributes were stored correctly.

Also notice how the test serves as micro-documentation for people using the API. It's an example of how to call addCamper and describes the expected behavior. In this case, the method should return a valid object and not nil.

Notice that this test creates the object and checks the attributes, but doesn't save anything to the store. This project uses a separate queue context so it can persist data in the background. However, the test runs straight through; this means you can't check for the save result with an XCTAssert as you can't be sure when the background operation has completed. Saving data is an important part of Core Data — so how can you test this part of the app?

Asynchronous tests

When using a single managed object context in Core Data, everything runs on the main UI thread. However, it's a common pattern to create background contexts, which are children of the main context, for doing work without blocking the UI.

Performing work on the correct thread for a given context is easy: You simply wrap the work in performBlockAndWait() or performBlock() to ensure it's executed on the thread associated with the context. performBlockAndWait() will wait to finish execution of the block before continuing, while performBlock() will immediately return and queue the execution on the context.

Testing performBlock() executions can be tricky since you need some way to send a signal about the test status to the outside world from inside the block. Luckily, there is a feature in XCTestCase called **expectations** that help with this.

The example below shows how you might use an expectation to wait for an asynchronous method to complete before finishing the test:

```
let expectation = expectation(withDescription: "Done!")

someService.callMethodWithCompletionHandler() {
  expectation.fulfill()
}

waitForExpectations(timeout: 2.0, handler: nil)
```

The key is that something must fulfill or trigger the expectation so the test moves forward. The wait method at the end takes a time parameter (in seconds) so the test doesn't wait forever and can time out (and fail) in case the expectation is never fulfilled.

In the example provided, `fulfill()` is called explicitly in the completion handler passed into the tested method. With Core Data save operations, it's easier to listen for the `NSManagedObjectContextDidSave` notification, since it happens in a place where you can't call `fulfill()` explicitly.

Add a new method to **CamperServiceTests.swift** to test that the root context is saved when you add a new camper:

```swift
func testRootContextIsSavedAfterAddingCamper() {
  //1
  let derivedContext = coreDataStack.newDerivedContext()
  camperService = CamperService(
    managedObjectContext: derivedContext,
    coreDataStack: coreDataStack)

  //2
  expectation(
    forNotification: .NSManagedObjectContextDidSave,
    object: coreDataStack.mainContext) {
      notification in
      return true
  }

  //3
  derivedContext.perform {
    let camper = self.camperService.addCamper("Bacon Lover",
      phoneNumber: "910-543-9000")
    XCTAssertNotNil(camper)
  }

  //4
  waitForExpectations(timeout: 2.0) { error in
    XCTAssertNil(error, "Save did not occur")
  }
}
```

Here's a breakdown of the code:

1. For this test, you create a background context to do the work. The `CamperService` instance is recreated using this context instead of the main context.

2. You create a text expectation linked to a notification. In this case, the expectation is linked to the NSManagedObjectContextDidSave notification from the root context of the Core Data stack. The handler for the notification is simple: it returns true since all you care about is that the notification is fired.

3. You add the camper, exactly the same as before, but this time inside a perform block on the derived context, since that's a background context and needs to run operations on its own thread.

4. The test waits up to two seconds for the expectation. If there's errors or the timeout passes, the error parameter for the handler block will contain a value.

Run the unit tests, and you should see a green checkmark next to this new method. It's important to keep UI-blocking operations such as Core Data save actions off the main thread so your app stays responsive.

Test expectations are invaluable to make sure these asynchronous operations are covered by unit tests.

You've added tests for existing features in the app; now it's time to add some features and tests yourself. Or for even more fun — perhaps write the tests first?

Tests first

An important function of CampgroundManager is its ability to reserve sites for campers. Before it can accept reservations, the system has to know about all of the campsites at the campground. CampSiteService was created to help with adding, deleting and finding campsites.

Open CampSiteService, and you'll notice that the only method implemented is addCampSite. There's no unit tests for this method, so create a test case for the service:

1. Right-click **Services** under the **CampgroundManagerTests** group and click **New File**.

2. Select **iOS\Source\Unit Test Case Class**. Click **Next**.

3. Name the class **CampSiteServiceTests**; subclass of **XCTestCase** should already be selected. Select **Swift** for the language, then click **Next**.

4. Make sure the **CampgroundManagerTests** target checkbox is the only target selected. Click **Create**.

Replace the contents of the file with the following:

```
import UIKit
import XCTest
import CampgroundManager
import CoreData

class CampSiteServiceTests: XCTestCase {

  // MARK: Properties
  var campSiteService: CampSiteService!
  var coreDataStack: CoreDataStack!

  override func setUp() {
    super.setUp()

    coreDataStack = TestCoreDataStack()
    campSiteService = CampSiteService(
      managedObjectContext: coreDataStack.mainContext,
      coreDataStack: coreDataStack)
  }

  override func tearDown() {
    super.tearDown()

    campSiteService = nil
    coreDataStack = nil
  }
}
```

This looks very similar to the previous test class. As your suite of tests expands and you notice common or repeated code, you can refactor your tests as well as your application code. You can feel safe doing this because the unit tests will fail if you mess anything up!

Add the following new method to test adding a campsite. This looks and works like the method for testing the creation of a new camper:

```
func testAddCampSite() {
  let campSite = campSiteService.addCampSite(1,
    electricity: true,
    water: true)

  XCTAssertTrue(campSite.siteNumber == 1,
    "Site number should be 1")
  XCTAssertTrue(campSite.electricity!.boolValue,
    "Site should have electricity")
  XCTAssertTrue(campSite.water!.boolValue,
    "Site should have water")
}
```

To ensure the context is saved during this method, add the following to test:

```swift
func testRootContextIsSavedAfterAddingCampsite() {
  let derivedContext = coreDataStack.newDerivedContext()

  campSiteService = CampSiteService(
    managedObjectContext: derivedContext,
    coreDataStack: coreDataStack)

  expectation(
    forNotification: .NSManagedObjectContextDidSave,
    object: coreDataStack.mainContext) {
      notification in
      return true
  }

  derivedContext.perform {
    let campSite = self.campSiteService.addCampSite(1,
      electricity: true,
      water: true)
    XCTAssertNotNil(campSite)
  }

  waitForExpectations(timeout: 2.0) { error in
    XCTAssertNil(error, "Save did not occur")
  }
}
```

This method should also look quite familiar to the ones you created earlier. Run the unit tests; everything should pass. At this point, you should be feeling a bit paranoid. What if the tests are broken and they *always* pass? It's time to do some test-driven development and get the buzz that comes from turning red tests to green!

> **Note**: Test-Driven Development (TDD) is a way of developing an application by writing a test first, then incrementally implementing the feature until the test passes. The code is then refactored for the next feature or improvement. Covering TDD methodologies is beyond the scope of this chapter, but the steps you're covering here will help you use TDD if you do decide to follow it.

Add the following methods to **CampSiteServiceTests.swift** to test getCampSite():

```swift
func testGetCampSiteWithMatchingSiteNumber() {
  _ = campSiteService.addCampSite(1,
    electricity: true,
    water: true)

  let campSite = campSiteService.getCampSite(1)
```

```
    XCTAssertNotNil(campSite, "A campsite should be returned")
}

func testGetCampSiteNoMatchingSiteNumber() {
  _ = campSiteService.addCampSite(1,
    electricity: true,
    water: true)

  let campSite = campSiteService.getCampSite(2)
  XCTAssertNil(campSite, "No campsite should be returned")
}
```

Both tests use the addCampSite method to create a new CampSite. You know this method works from your previous test, so there's no need to test it again. The actual tests cover retrieving the CampSite by ID and testing whether the result is nil.

Think about how more reliable it is to start every test with an empty database. If you weren't using the in-memory store, there could easily be a campsite matching the ID for the second test, which would then fail!

Run the unit tests. The test expecting a CampSite fails because you haven't implemented getCampSite yet.

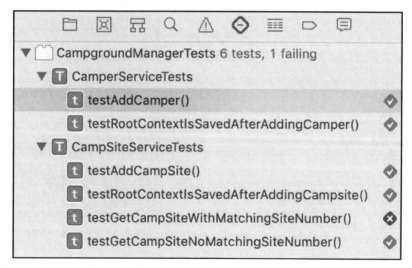

The other unit test — the one that expects no site — passes. This is an example of a false positive, because the method always returns nil. It's important that you add tests for multiple scenarios for each method to exercise as many code paths as possible.

Implement `getCampSite` in **CampSiteService.swift** with the following code:

```
public func getCampSite(_ siteNumber: NSNumber) -> CampSite? {
  let fetchRequest: NSFetchRequest<CampSite> =
    CampSite.fetchRequest()
  fetchRequest.predicate =
    NSPredicate(format: "%K = %@",
                argumentArray: [#keyPath(CampSite.siteNumber),
                                siteNumber])

  let results: [CampSite]?
  do {
    results = try managedObjectContext.fetch(fetchRequest)
  } catch {
    return nil
  }

  return results?.first
}
```

Now rerun the unit tests and you should see green check marks. Ah, the sweet satisfaction of success!

> **Note**: The final project for this chapter included in the resources bundled with this book includes unit tests covering multiple scenarios for each method. You can browse through that code for even more examples.

Validation and refactoring

`ReservationService` will contain some fairly complex logic to figure out if a camper is able to reserve a site. The unit tests for `ReservationService` will require every service created so far to test its operation.

Create a new test class as you've done before:

1. Right-click **Services** under the **CampgroundManagerTests** group and click **New File**.

2. Select **iOS ▸ Source ▸ Unit Test Case Class**. Click **Next**.

3. Name the class **ReservationServiceTests**; subclass of **XCTestCase** should already be selected. Select **Swift** for the language. Click **Next**.

4. Make sure the **CampgroundManagerTests** target checkbox is the only target selected. Click **Create**.

Replace the contents of the file with the following:

```
import Foundation
import CoreData
import XCTest
import CampgroundManager

class ReservationServiceTests: XCTestCase {

  // MARK: Properties
  var campSiteService: CampSiteService!
  var camperService: CamperService!
  var reservationService: ReservationService!
  var coreDataStack: CoreDataStack!

  override func setUp() {
    super.setUp()
    coreDataStack = TestCoreDataStack()
    camperService = CamperService(
      managedObjectContext: coreDataStack.mainContext,
      coreDataStack: coreDataStack)
    campSiteService = CampSiteService(
      managedObjectContext: coreDataStack.mainContext,
      coreDataStack: coreDataStack)
    reservationService = ReservationService(
      managedObjectContext: coreDataStack.mainContext,
      coreDataStack: coreDataStack)
  }

  override func tearDown() {
    super.tearDown()

    camperService = nil
    campSiteService = nil
    reservationService = nil
    coreDataStack = nil
  }
}
```

This is a slightly longer version of the set up and tear down code you've used in the previous test case classes. Along with setting up the Core Data stack as usual, you're creating a fresh instance of each service in setUp for each test.

Add the following method to test creating a reservation:

```
func testReserveCampSitePositiveNumberOfDays() {
  let camper = camperService.addCamper("Johnny Appleseed",
    phoneNumber: "408-555-1234")!
```

```
    let campSite = campSiteService.addCampSite(15,
      electricity: false,
      water: false)

    let result = reservationService.reserveCampSite(campSite,
      camper: camper,
      date: Date(),
      numberOfNights: 5)

  XCTAssertNotNil(result.reservation,
    "Reservation should not be nil")
  XCTAssertNil(result.error,
    "No error should be present")
  XCTAssertTrue(result.reservation?.status == "Reserved",
    "Status should be Reserved")
}
```

The unit test creates a camper and campsite, both required to reserve a site. The new part here is you're using the reservation service to reserve the campsite, linking the camper and campsite together with a date.

The unit test verifies that a Reservation object was created and an NSError object wasn't in the returned tuple. Looking at the reserveCampSite call, you've probably realized the number of nights should be at least greater than zero. Add the following unit test to test that condition:

```
func testReserveCampSiteNegativeNumberOfDays() {
  let camper = camperService.addCamper("Johnny Appleseed",
    phoneNumber: "408-555-1234")!
  let campSite = campSiteService.addCampSite(15,
    electricity: false,
    water: false)

  let result = reservationService!.reserveCampSite(campSite,
    camper: camper,
    date: Date(),
    numberOfNights: -1)

  XCTAssertNotNil(result.reservation,
    "Reservation should not be nil")
  XCTAssertNotNil(result.error,
    "An error should be present")
  XCTAssertTrue(result.error?.userInfo["Problem"] as? String
    == "Invalid number of days",
    "Error problem should be present")
  XCTAssertTrue(result.reservation?.status == "Invalid",
    "Status should be Invalid")
}
```

Run the unit test, and you'll notice that the test fails. Apparently whoever wrote `ReservationService` didn't think to check for this! It's a good thing you caught that bug here in a test before it made it out into the world — maybe booking a negative number of nights would cascade down to issuing a refund!

Tests are great places for probing your system and finding holes in its behavior. The test also serves as a quasi-specification; the tests indicate you're still expecting a valid, non-`nil` result, but one with the error condition set.

Open **ReservationService.swift** and add the check for `numberOfNights` to `reserveCampSite`. Replace the line `reservation.status = "Reserved"` with the following:

```
if numberOfNights <= 0 {
  reservation.status = "Invalid"
  registrationError = NSError(domain: "CampingManager",
    code: 5,
    userInfo: ["Problem": "Invalid number of days"])
} else {
  reservation.status = "Reserved"
}
```

Finally, change `registrationError` from a constant to a variable by replacing `let` with `var`.

Now rerun the tests and check that the negative number of days test passes. You can see how the process continues with refactoring when you want to add additional functionality or validation rules.

Whether you know the details of the code you're testing or you're treating it like a black box, you can write these kinds of tests against the API to see if it behaves as you expect. If it does, great! That means the test will ensure your code functions as expected. If not, you either need to change your test to match the code, or change the code to match the test.

Key points

- Unit tests should follow the **FIRST** principles: Fast, Isolated, Repeatable, Self-verifying, and Timely.

- Create a persistent store specific for unit testing and reset its contents with every test. Using an in-memory store is the simplest approach.

- Core Data can be used asynchronously and is easily tested with the XCTestExpectation class.

Where to go from here?

You've probably heard many times that unit testing your work is key in maintaining a stable software product. While Core Data can help eliminate a lot of error-prone persistence code from your project, it can be a source of logic errors if used incorrectly.

Writing unit tests that can use Core Data will help stabilize your code before it even reaches your users. XCTestExpectation is a simple, yet powerful tool in your quest to test Core Data in an asynchronous manner. Use it wisely!

As a challenge, CampSiteService has a number of methods that are not implemented yet, marked with TODO comments. Using a TDD approach, write unit tests and then implement the methods to make the tests pass. If you get stuck, check out the challenge project included in the resources for this chapter for a sample solution.

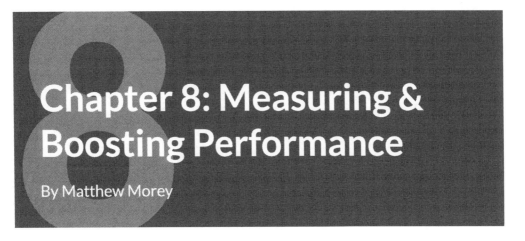

Chapter 8: Measuring & Boosting Performance

By Matthew Morey

In many ways, it's a no-brainer: You should strive to optimize the performance of any app you develop. An app with poor performance will, at best, receive bad reviews and, at worst, become unresponsive and crash.

This is no less true of apps that use Core Data. Luckily, most implementations of Core Data are fast and light already, due to Core Data's built-in optimizations, such as faulting.

However, the flexibility that makes Core Data a great tool means you can use it in ways that negatively impact performance. From poor choices in setting up the data model to inefficient fetching and searching, there are many opportunities for Core Data to slow down your app.

You'll begin the chapter with an app that's a slow-working memory hog. By the end of the chapter, you'll have an app that's light and fast, and you'll know exactly where to look and what to do if you find yourself with your own heavy, sluggish app — and how to avoid that situation in the first place!

Getting started

As with most things, performance is a balance between memory and speed. Your app's Core Data model objects can exist in two places: in random access memory (RAM) or on disk.

Accessing data in RAM is much faster than accessing data on disk, but devices have much less RAM than disk space.

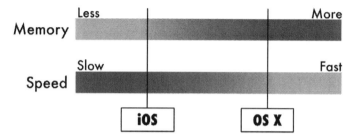

iOS devices, in particular, have less available RAM, which prevents you from loading tons of data into memory. With fewer model objects in RAM, your app's operations will be slower due to frequent slow disk access. As you load more model objects into RAM, your app will probably feel more responsive, but you can't starve out other apps or the OS will terminate your app!

The starter project

The starter project, EmployeeDirectory, is a tab bar-based app full of employee information. It's like the Contacts app, but for a single fictional company.

Open the EmployeeDirectory starter project for this chapter in Xcode and build and run it.

The app will take a long time to launch and once it does launch, it will feel sluggish and may even crash as you use it. Rest assured, this is by design!

> **Note**: It's possible the starter project may not even launch on your system. The app was architected to be as sluggish as possible while still able to run on most systems, so the performance improvements you'll make will be easily noticeable. If the app refuses to work on your system, continue to follow along. The first set of changes you make should enable the app to work on even the slowest devices.

As you can see in the following screenshots, the first tab includes a table view and a custom cell with basic information, such as name and department, for all employees.

Tap a cell to reveal more details for the selected employee, such as start date and remaining vacation days.

Tap the profile picture of the employee makes the picture full-screen; tap anywhere on the full-screen picture to dismiss it.

The startup time of the app is quite long, and the scrolling performance of the initial employee list could use some work. The app also uses a lot of memory, which you'll measure yourself in the next section.

Measure, change, verify

Instead of guessing where your performance bottlenecks are, you can save yourself time and effort by first measuring your app's performance in targeted ways. Xcode provides tools just for this purpose.

Ideally, you should measure performance, make targeted changes and then measure again to validate your changes had the intended impact.

You should repeat this measure–change–verify process as many times as needed until your app meets all of your performance requirements.

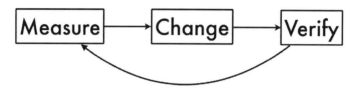

In this chapter, you'll do just that:

- You'll measure performance issues in the provided starter project using Gauges, Instruments and the XCTest framework.

- Next, you'll make changes to the code that will improve the performance of the app.

- Finally, you'll verify the changes had the intended results by measuring again.

You'll then repeat this cycle until EmployeeDirectory performs like a Core Data champ!

Measuring the problem

Build, run, and wait for the app to launch. Once it does, use the **Memory Report** to view how much RAM the app is using.

To launch the Memory Report, first verify that the app is running and then perform the following steps:

1. Click on the **Debug navigator** in the left navigator pane.

2. To get more information, expand the **running process** — in this case, **EmployeeDirectory** — by tapping on the arrow.

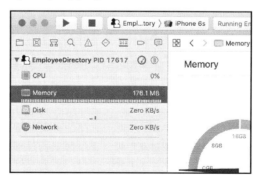

Now, click on the **Memory** row and look at the top half of the memory gauge:

The top half includes a **Memory Use** gauge showing the amount and percentage of memory your app is using. For EmployeeDirectory, you'll see about 135 MB of memory is in use, or about 7% of the available RAM on an iPhone 6S, which is the least-performant device that still runs iOS 13.

The **Usage Comparison** pie chart depicts this chunk of memory as a fraction of the total available memory. It also shows the amount of RAM in use by other processes, as well as the amount of available free RAM, which in this case is 329.2 MB.

Now, look at the bottom half of the Memory Report:

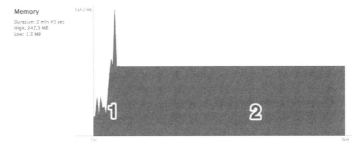

The bottom half consists of a chart showing RAM usage over time. For EmployeeDirectory, you'll see two distinct areas.

1. Upon first launch, EmployeeDirectory performs an import operation before loading the primary employee list. Ignore these spikes in memory for now.

2. The next chunk of memory usage takes place after the import operation, when the employee list is visible. Once the app has fully loaded the list, you can see the memory usage is fairly stable.

> **Note**: If you use a device besides an iPhone 6S or iPhone SE, including the iOS Simulator, your memory gauge may not look exactly like these screenshots. The utilization percentages will be based off of the amount of available RAM on your test device, which may not match the RAM available on an iPhone 6S.

The RAM usage is quite high, considering there's only 50 employee records in the app. The data model itself could be at fault here, so that's where you'll start your investigation.

Exploring the data source

In Xcode, open the project navigator and click on **EmployeeDirectory.xcdatamodeld** to view the data model. The model for the starter project consists of an Employee entity with 11 attributes and a Sale entity with two attributes.

On the Employee entity, the about, address, department, email, guid, name and phone attributes are string types; active is a Boolean; picture is binary data; startDate is a date and vacationDays is an integer. Employee has a *to-many* relationship with Sale, which contains an amount integer attribute and a date Date attribute.

On first launch, the app will import sample data from the bundled JSON file **seed.json**. Here's an excerpt of the JSON:

```
{
  "guid": "769adb89-82ad-4b39-be41-d02b89de7b94",
  "active": true,
  "picture": "face10.jpg",
  "name": "Kasey Mcfarland",
  "vacationDays": 2,
  "department": "Marketing",
  "startDate": "1979-09-05",
  "email": "kaseymcfarland@liquicom.com",
  "phone": "+1 (909) 561-2981",
  "address": "201 Lancaster Avenue, West Virginia, 2583",
  "about": "Dolore reprehenderit ... voluptate consectetur.\r\n"
},
```

Note: You can vary the amount and type of data the app imports from the **seed.json** file by modifying the amountToImport and addSalesRecords constants located at the top of **AppDelegate.swift**. For now, leave these constants set to their default values.

In terms of performance, the text showing the employee names, departments, email addresses and phone numbers is inconsequential compared to the size of the profile pictures, which are large enough to potentially impact the performance of the list.

Now that you've measured the problem and have a baseline for future comparisons, you'll make changes to the data model to reduce the amount of RAM in use.

Making changes to improve performance

The likely culprit for the high memory usage is the employee profile picture. Since the picture is stored as a binary data attribute, Core Data will allocate memory and load the entire picture when you access an employee record — even if you only need to access the employee's name or email address!

The solution here is to split out the picture into a separate, related record. In theory, you'll be able to access the employee record efficiently, and then take the hit for loading the picture only when you really need it.

To start, open the visual model editor by clicking on **EmployeeDirectory.xcdatamodeld**. Start by creating an object, or entity, in your model. In the bottom toolbar, click the **Add Entity** plus (+) button to add a new entity.

Name the entity **EmployeePicture**. Then click the entity and make sure the fourth tab is selected in the Utilities section. Change the class to **EmployeePicture**, Module to **Current Product Module** and Codegen to **Manual/None**.

Make sure the **EmployeePicture** entity is selected by clicking on either the entity name in the left panel or the diagram for the entity in the diagram view.

Next, click and hold on the plus (+) button in the lower-right (next to the Editor Style segmented control) and then click **Add Attribute** from the popup. Name the new attribute **picture**.

Finally, in the data model inspector, change the **Attribute Type** to **Binary Data** and check the **Allows External** Storage option.

Your editor should look like this:

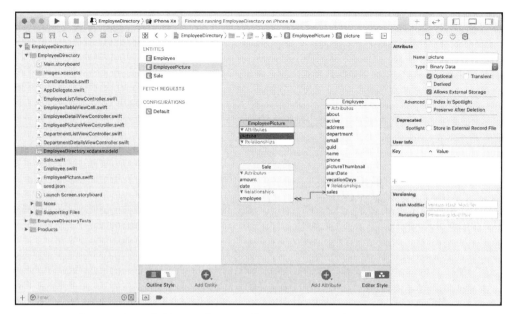

As previously mentioned, binary data attributes are usually stored right in the database. If you check the **Allows External Storage** option, Core Data automatically decides if it's better to save the data to disk as a separate file or leave it in the SQLite database.

Select the Employee entity and rename the **picture** attribute to **pictureThumbnail**. To do so, select the picture attribute in the diagram view and then edit the name in the data model inspector.

You've updated the model to store the original picture in a separate entity and a thumbnail version on the main Employee entity. The smaller thumbnail pictures won't require as much RAM when the app fetches Employee entities from Core Data. Once you've finished modifying the rest of the project, you'll get a chance to test this out and verify the app is using less RAM than before.

You can link the two entities together with a relationship. That way, when the app needs the higher-quality, larger picture, it can still retrieve it via a relationship.

Select the **Employee** entity and click and hold the plus (+) button in the lower right. This time, select **Add Relationship**. Name the relationship **picture**, set the destination as **EmployeePicture** and finally, set the **Delete Rule** to **Cascade**.

Core Data relationships should always go both ways, so now add a corresponding relationship. Select the **EmployeePicture** entity and add a new relationship. Name the new relationship **employee**, set the **Destination** to **Employee** and finally, set the **Inverse** to **picture**.

Your model should now look like this:

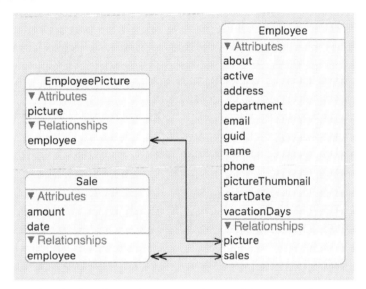

Now that you've finished making changes to the model, you need to create an NSManagedObject subclass for the new EmployeePicture entity. This subclass will let you access the new entity from code.

Right-click on the **EmployeeDirectory** group folder and select **New File**. Select the **Cocoa Touch Class** template and click **Next**. Name the class **EmployeePicture** and make it a subclass of **NSManagedObject**. Make sure **Swift** is selected for the **Language**, click **Next** and finally click **Create**.

Select **EmployeePicture.swift** from the project navigator and replace the automatically generated code with the following code:

```swift
import Foundation
import CoreData

public class EmployeePicture: NSManagedObject {
}

extension EmployeePicture {
  @nonobjc public class func fetchRequest() ->
    NSFetchRequest<EmployeePicture> {
    return NSFetchRequest<EmployeePicture>(
```

```
        entityName: "EmployeePicture")
  }

  @NSManaged public var picture: Data?
  @NSManaged public var employee: Employee?
}
```

This is a very simple class with just two properties. The first, **picture**, matches the single attribute on the **EmployeePicture** entity you just created in the visual data model editor. The second property, **employee**, matches the relationship you created on the **EmployeePicture** entity.

> **Note**: You could also have Xcode create the **EmployeePicture** class automatically. To add a new class this way, open **EmployeeDirectory.xcdatamodeld**, go to **Editor ▸ Create NSManagedObject Subclass…**, select the data model and then select the **EmployeePicture** entity in the next two dialog boxes. Select **Swift** as the language option in the final box. If you're asked, say **No** to creating an Objective-C bridging header. Click **Create** to save the file.

Next, select the **Employee.swift** file from the project navigator and update the code to make use of the new **pictureThumbnail** attribute and **picture** relationship. Rename the picture variable to `pictureThumbnail` and add a new variable named `picture` of type `EmployeePicture`. Your variables will now look like this:

```
@NSManaged public var about: String?
@NSManaged public var active: NSNumber?
@NSManaged public var address: String?
@NSManaged public var department: String?
@NSManaged public var email: String?
@NSManaged public var guid: String?
@NSManaged public var name: String?
@NSManaged public var phone: String?
@NSManaged public var pictureThumbnail: Data?
@NSManaged public var picture: EmployeePicture?
@NSManaged public var startDate: Date?
@NSManaged public var vacationDays: NSNumber?
@NSManaged public var sales: NSSet?
```

Next, you need to update the rest of the app to make use of the new entities and attributes.

Open **EmployeeListViewController.swift** and find the following lines of code in `tableView(_:cellForRowAt:)`.

It should be easy to find, as it will have an error marker next to it!

```
cell.pictureImageView.image = UIImage(data: employee.picture!)
```

This code sets the picture on the cell in the employee list. Now the full picture is held in a separate entity, you should use the newly added `pictureThumbnail` attribute. Update the file to match the following code:

```
cell.pictureImageView.image =
    UIImage(data: employee.pictureThumbnail!)
```

Now open **EmployeeDetailViewController.swift** and find the following code within `configureView()`. Again, it should be showing an error:

```
let image = UIImage(data: employee.picture!)
headShotImageView.image = image
```

You'll need to update the picture that's set, just as you did in **EmployeeListViewController.swift**. Like the cell picture, the employee detail view will only have a small picture and therefore only needs the thumbnail version. Update the code to look like the following:

```
let image = UIImage(data: employee.pictureThumbnail!)
headShotImageView.image = image
```

Open **EmployeePictureViewController.swift** and find the following code in `configureView()`:

```
guard let employeePicture = employee?.picture else {
  return
}
```

This time, you want to use the high-quality version of the picture, since the image will be shown full-screen. Update the file to use the **picture** relationship you created on the **Employee** entity to access the high-quality version of the picture:

```
guard let employeePicture = employee?.picture?.picture else {
  return
}
```

There's one more thing to do before you build and run. Open **AppDelegate.swift** and find the following line of code in `importJSONSeedData(_:)`:

```
employee.picture = pictureData
```

Now that you have a separate entity for storing the high-quality picture, you need to update this line of code to set the `pictureThumbnail` attribute and the `picture` relationship.

Replace the line above with the following:

```
employee.pictureThumbnail =
    imageDataScaledToHeight(pictureData, height: 120)

let pictureObject =
    EmployeePicture(context: coreDataStack.mainContext)

pictureObject.picture = pictureData

employee.picture = pictureObject
```

First, you use `imageDataScaledToHeight` to set the `pictureThumbnail` to a smaller version of the original picture. Next, you create a new `EmployeePicture` entity.

You set the `picture` attribute on the new `EmployeePicture` entity to the `pictureData` constant. Finally, you set the `picture` relationship on the `employee` entity to the newly-created `picture` entity.

> **Note**: imageDataScaledToHeight takes in image data, resizes it to the passed-in height and sets the quality to 80% before returning the new image data.

If you have an app that needs pictures and retrieves data via a network call, you should make sure the API doesn't already include smaller thumbnail versions of the pictures. There's a small performance cost associated with converting images on the fly like this.

Since you changed the model, delete the app from your testing device. Now build and run. Give it a go! You should see exactly what you saw before:

The app should work as before, and you might even notice a small performance difference because of the thumbnails. But the main reason for this change was to improve memory usage.

Verify the changes

Now that you've made all the necessary changes to the project, it's time to see if you actually improved the app.

While the app is running, use the **Memory Report** to view how much RAM the app is using. This time it's consumed only about 41 MB of RAM, or about 2% of the total available RAM of the iPhone 6S.

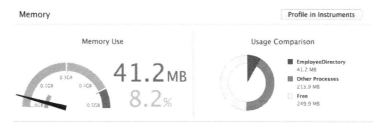

Now look at the bottom half of the report. Like last time, the initial spike is from the import operation and you can ignore it. The flat area is much lower this time.

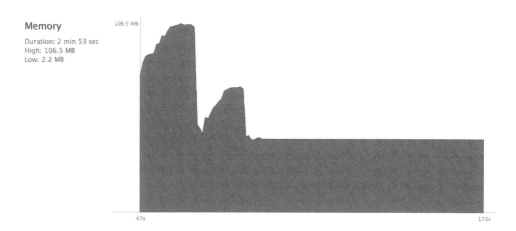

Congratulations, you've reduced this app's RAM usage simply by making adjustments to its data model!

First, you **measured** the app's performance using the Memory Report tool. Next, you made **changes** to the way Core Data stores and accesses the app's data. Finally, you **verified** the changes improved the app's performance.

Fetching and performance

Core Data is the keeper of your app's data. Anytime you want to access the data, you have to retrieve it with a fetch request.

For example, when the app loads the employee list, it needs to perform a fetch. But each trip to the persistent store incurs overhead. You don't want to fetch more data than you need — just enough so you aren't constantly going back to disk. Remember, disk access is much slower than RAM access.

For maximum performance, you need to strike a balance between the number of objects you fetch at any given time and the usefulness of having many records taking up valuable space in RAM.

The startup time of the app is a little slow, suggesting something is going on with the initial fetch.

Fetch batch size

Core Data fetch requests include the fetchBatchSize property, which makes it easy to fetch just enough data, but not too much.

If you don't set a batch size, Core Data uses the default value of 0, which disables batching.

Setting a non-zero positive batch size lets you limit the amount of data returned to the batch size. As the app needs more data, Core Data automatically performs more batch operations. If you searched the source code of the EmployeeDirectory app, you wouldn't see any calls to `fetchBatchSize`. This indicates another potential area for improvement!

Let's see if there's any places you could use a batch size to improve the app's performance.

Measuring the problem

You'll use the **Instruments** tool to analyze where the fetch operations are in your app.

First, select one of the iPhone simulator targets and then from Xcode's menu bar, select **Product** and then **Profile** (or press ⌘ + I). This will build the app and launch Instruments.

> **Note**: You can only use the Instruments Core Data template with the Simulator, as the template requires the DTrace tool which is not available on real iOS devices. You may also need to select a development team for the Target to enable Instruments to run.

You'll be greeted by the following selection window:

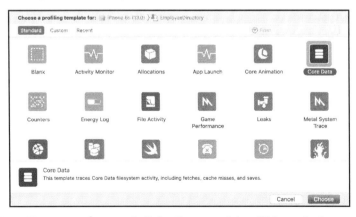

Select the **Core Data** template and click **Choose**. This will launch the Instruments window. If this is the first time you've launched Instruments, you might be asked for your password to authorize Instruments to analyze running processes — don't worry, it's safe to enter your password in this dialog.

Once Instruments has launched, click on the **Record** button in the top-left of the window.

Once EmployeeDirectory has launched, scroll up and down the employee list for about 20 seconds and then click on the **Stop** button that's appeared in place of the Record button.

Click on the **Fetches** tool. The Instruments window should now look like this:

The default Core Data template includes the following tools to help you tune and monitor performance:

- **Faults Instrument**: Captures information about fault events that result in cache misses. This can help diagnose performance in low-memory situations.

- **Fetches Instrument**: Captures fetch count and duration of fetch operations. This will help you balance the number of fetch requests versus the size of each request.

- **Saves Instrument**: Captures information on managed object context save events. Writing data out to disk can be a performance and battery hit, so this instrument can help you determine whether you should batch things into one big save rather than many small ones.

Since you clicked on the Fetches tool, the details section at the bottom of the Instruments window shows more information about each fetch that occurred.

Each of the three rows corresponds to the same line of code in the app. The first two rows are private Core Data calls generated by lines of code in the app, so you can ignore them.

Pay attention to the last row, though. This row includes the Objective-C versions of the **caller**, **fetch count** and **fetch duration** in microseconds.

EmployeeDirectory imports 50 employees. The fetch count shows 50, which means the app is fetching *all* employees from Core Data at the same time. That's not very efficient!

The Fetches tool corroborates your experience, the fetch is slow and it's easily noticeable, as you can see it takes about 5,000 microseconds. The app has to complete this fetch before it makes the table view visible and ready for user interaction.

> **Note**: Depending on your Mac, the numbers onscreen (and the thickness of the bars) might not match those shown in these screenshots. Faster Macs will have quicker fetches. Don't worry — what's important is the change in time you'll see after you modify the project.

Changes to improve performance

Open **EmployeeListViewController.swift** and find the following line of code in employeeFetchRequest(_:):

```
let fetchRequest: NSFetchRequest<Employee> =
    Employee.fetchRequest()
```

This code creates a fetch request using the **Employee** entity. You haven't set a batch size, so it defaults to 0, which means no batching. Now set the batch size on the fetch request to 10, replace the above with the following:

```
let fetchRequest: NSFetchRequest<Employee> =
    Employee.fetchRequest()
fetchRequest.fetchBatchSize = 10
```

How do you come up with an optimal batch size? A good rule of thumb is to set the batch size to about double the number of items that appear onscreen at any given time. The employee list shows three to five employees onscreen at once, so 10 is a reasonable batch size.

Verify the changes

Now that you've made the necessary change to the project, it's once again time to see if you've actually improved the app.

To test this fix, first build and run the app and make sure it still works.

Next launch Instruments again: from Xcode, select **Product** and then **Profile**, or press ⌘ + I) and repeat the steps you followed previously. Remember to scroll up and down the employee list for about **20 seconds** before clicking the **Stop** button in Instruments.

> **Note**: To use the latest code, make sure you launch the app from Xcode, which triggers a build, rather than just hitting the red button in Instruments.

This time, the Core Data Instrument should look like this:

Now there are multiple fetches, and the initial fetch is faster!

Examine the detail section more closely.

Again, instead of a single fetch, you see multiple quicker fetches.

The first fetch looks similar to the original fetch, as it is fetching all 50 employees. This time, however, it's only fetching the count of the objects, instead of the full objects, which makes the fetch duration much shorter. Core Data does this automatically, now that you've set a batch size on the request.

Looking at the results on my system, this fetch originally took over 5,000 microseconds, and now it only takes about 2,000 microseconds.

After the first fetch, you can see numerous fetches in batches of 10. As you scroll through the employee list, new entities are fetched only when needed.

You've cut the time of the initial fetch down to almost a third of the original, and the subsequent fetches are much smaller and faster. Congratulations, you have increased the speed of your app again!

Advanced fetching

Fetch requests use predicates to limit the amount of data returned. As mentioned above, for optimal performance, you should limit the amount of data you fetch to the minimum needed: the more data you fetch, the longer the fetch will take.

> **Fetch Predicate Performance**: You can limit your fetch requests by using predicates. If your fetch request requires a compound predicate, you can make it more efficient by putting the more restrictive predicate first. This is especially true if your predicate contains string comparisons. For example, a predicate with a format of `"(active == YES) AND (name CONTAINS[cd] %@)"` would likely be more efficient than `"(name CONTAINS[cd] %@) AND (active == YES)"`.
>
> For more predicate performance optimizations please consult Apple's Predicate Programming Guide: apple.co/2a1Rq2n.

Build and run EmployeeDirectory, and select the second tab labeled Departments. This tab shows a listing of departments and the number of employees in each department.

Tap a department cell to see a list of the employees in the selected department.

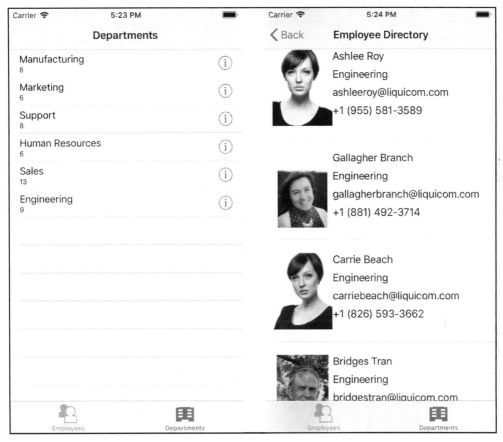

Tap the detail disclosure, also known as the information icon, in each department cell to show the total employees, active employees and a breakdown of employees' available vacations days.

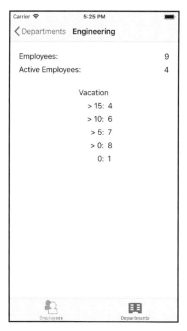

The first screen simply lists the departments and the number of employees per department. There's not too much data here, but there could still be performance issues lurking here. Let's find out.

Measure the problem

Instead of Instruments, you'll use the **XCTest** framework to measure the performance of the department list screen. XCTest is usually used for unit tests, but it also contains useful tools for testing performance.

> **Note**: For more information on unit tests and Core Data, check out Chapter 7, "Unit Testing".

First, familiarize yourself with how the app creates the department list screen. Open **DepartmentListViewController.swift** and find the following code in `totalEmployeesPerDepartment()`.

```
//1
let fetchRequest: NSFetchRequest<Employee> =
Employee.fetchRequest()

var fetchResults: [Employee] = []
do {
```

```
    fetchResults = try
  coreDataStack.mainContext.fetch(fetchRequest)
  } catch let error as NSError {
    print("ERROR: \(error.localizedDescription)")
    return [[String: String]]()
  }

  //2
  var uniqueDepartments: [String: Int] = [:]
  for employee in fetchResults where employee.department != nil {
    uniqueDepartments[employee.department!, default: 0] += 1
  }

  //3
  return uniqueDepartments.map { (department, headCount) in
    ["department": department,
      "headCount": String(headCount)]
  }
}
```

This code does the following:

1. It creates a fetch request with the Employee entity and then fetches all employees.

2. It iterates though the employees and builds a dictionary, where the key is the department name and the value is the number of employees in that department.

3. It builds an array of dictionaries with the required information for the department list screen.

Now to measure the performance of this code.

Open **DepartmentListViewControllerTests.swift** (notice the Tests suffix in the filename) and add the following method:

```
func testTotalEmployeesPerDepartment() {
  measureMetrics([.wallClockTime],
             automaticallyStartMeasuring: false) {

    let departmentList = DepartmentListViewController()
    departmentList.coreDataStack =
      CoreDataStack(modelName: "EmployeeDirectory")

    startMeasuring()
    _ = departmentList.totalEmployeesPerDepartment()
    stopMeasuring()
  }
}
```

This function uses `measureMetrics` to see how long code takes to execute.

You have to set up a new Core Data stack each time so your results don't get skewed by Core Data's excellent caching abilities, which would make subsequent test runs really fast!

Inside the block, you first create a `DepartmentListViewController` and give it a `CoreDataStack`. Then, you call `totalEmployeesPerDepartment` to retrieve the number of employees per department.

Now you need to run this test. From Xcode's menu bar, select **Product** and then **Test**, or press ⌘ + U. This will build the app and run the tests.

Once the tests have finished running, Xcode will look like this:

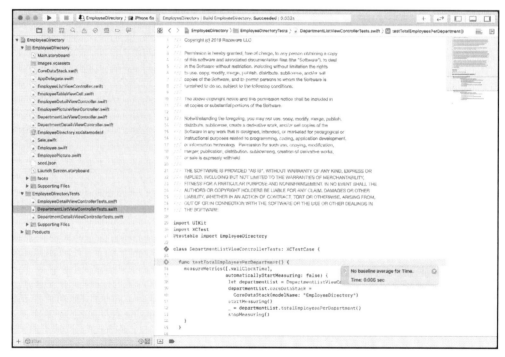

Notice two new things:

1. There's a green checkmark next to `testTotalEmployeesPerDepartment`. That means the test ran and passed.

2. There's a message on the right side with the amount of time the test took.

On the low-spec test device used for the above screenshot, the test took 0.252 seconds to perform the `totalEmployeesPerDepartment` operation. These results might seem good, but there is still room for improvement.

> **Note**: You might get somewhat different test results, depending on your test device. Don't worry — what's important is the change in time you'll see after you modify the project.

Changes to improve performance

The current implementation of `totalEmployeesPerDepartment` uses a fetch request to iterate through all employee records. Remember the very first optimization in this chapter, where you split out the full-size photo into a separate entity? There's a similar issue here: Core Data loads the entire employee record, but all you really need is a count of employees by department.

It would be more efficient to somehow group the records by department and count them. You don't need details like employee names and photo thumbnails!

Open **DepartmentListViewController.swift** and add the following code to the class below `totalEmployeesPerDepartment()`:

```swift
func totalEmployeesPerDepartmentFast() -> [[String: String]] {
  //1
  let expressionDescription = NSExpressionDescription()
  expressionDescription.name = "headCount"

  //2
  let arguments = [NSExpression(forKeyPath: "department")]
  expressionDescription.expression =
    NSExpression(forFunction: "count:",
                 arguments: arguments)

  //3
  let fetchRequest: NSFetchRequest<NSDictionary> =
    NSFetchRequest(entityName: "Employee")
  fetchRequest.propertiesToFetch =
    ["department", expressionDescription]
  fetchRequest.propertiesToGroupBy = ["department"]
  fetchRequest.resultType = .dictionaryResultType

  //4
  var fetchResults: [NSDictionary] = []
  do {
    fetchResults =
      try coreDataStack.mainContext.fetch(fetchRequest)
```

```
    } catch let error as NSError {
      print("ERROR: \(error.localizedDescription)")
      return [[String: String]]()
    }
    return fetchResults as! [[String: String]]
  }
```

This code still uses a fetch request to populate the department list screen, but it takes advantage of an NSExpression. Here's how it works:

1. First, you create a NSExpressionDescription and name it headCount.

2. Next, you create a NSExpression with the count: function for the department attribute.

3. Next, you create a fetch request with the Employee entity. This time, the fetch request should only fetch the minimum required properties by using propertiesToFetch; you only need the department attribute and the calculated property the expression created earlier. The fetch request also groups the results by the department attribute. You're not interested in the managed object, so the fetch request return type is DictionaryResultType. This will return an array of dictionaries, each containing a department name and an employee count — just what you need!

4. Finally, you execute the fetch request.

Find the following line of code in viewDidLoad():

```
    items = totalEmployeesPerDepartment()
```

This line of code uses the old and slow function to populate the department list screen. Replace it by calling the function you just created:

```
    items = totalEmployeesPerDepartmentFast()
```

Now the app populates the table view data source for the department list screen with the faster, NSExpression-backed fetch request.

> **Note**: NSExpression is a powerful API, yet it is seldom used, at least directly. When you create predicates with comparison operations, you may not know it, but you're actually using expressions. There are many pre-built statistical and arithmetical expressions available in NSExpression, including average, sum, count, min, max, median, mode and stddev.

> Consult the NSExpression documentation for a comprehensive overview.

Verify the changes

Now that you've made all the necessary changes to the project, it's once again time to see if you've improved the app's performance.

Open **DepartmentListViewControllerTests.swift** and add a new function to test the `totalEmployeesPerDepartmentFast` function you just created.

```swift
func testTotalEmployeesPerDepartmentFast() {
  measureMetrics([.wallClockTime],
                 automaticallyStartMeasuring: false) {
    let departmentList = DepartmentListViewController()
    departmentList.coreDataStack =
      CoreDataStack(modelName: "EmployeeDirectory")

    startMeasuring()
    _ = departmentList.totalEmployeesPerDepartmentFast()
    stopMeasuring()
  }
}
```

As before, this test uses `measureMetrics` to see how long a particular function is taking; in this case, `totalEmployeesPerDepartmentFast`.

Now you need to run this test. From Xcode's menu bar, select **Product** and then **Test**, or press ⌘ + **U**. This will build the app and run the tests. Once the tests have finished running, Xcode will look similar to the following:

This time, you'll see two messages with total execution time, one next to each test function.

> **Note**: If you don't see the time messages, you can view the details of each individual test run in the logs generated during the test. From Xcode's menu bar, select **View**, **Debug Area**, and then **Show Debug Area**.

Depending on your test device, the new function, `totalEmployeesPerDepartmentFast`, will take approximately 0.002 seconds to complete. That's much faster than the 0.1 to 0.3 seconds used by the original function, `totalEmployeesPerDepartment`. You've increased the speed by over 100%!

Fetching counts

As you've already seen, your app doesn't always need all information from your Core Data objects; some screens simply need the counts of objects that have certain attributes.

For example, the employee detail screen shows the total number of sales an employee has made since they've been with the company.

For the purposes of this app, you don't care about the content of each individual sale — for example, the date of the sale or the name of the purchaser — only how many sales there are in total.

Measure the problem

You'll use XCTest again to measure the performance of the employee detail screen.

Open **EmployeeDetailViewController.swift** and find
`salesCountForEmployee(_:)`.

```swift
func salesCountForEmployee(_ employee: Employee) -> String {

  let fetchRequest: NSFetchRequest<Sale> = Sale.fetchRequest()
  fetchRequest.predicate = NSPredicate(
    format: "%K = %@",
    argumentArray: [#keyPath(Sale.employee), employee])

  let context = employee.managedObjectContext!
  do {
    let results = try context.fetch(fetchRequest)
    return "\(results.count)"
  } catch let error as NSError {
    print("Error: \(error.localizedDescription)")
    return "0"
  }
}
```

This code fetches all sales for a given employee and then returns the count of the returned array.

Fetching the full sale object just to see how many sales exist for a given employee is probably wasteful. This might be another opportunity to boost performance!

Let's measure the problem before attempting to fix it.

Open **EmployeeDetailViewControllerTests.swift** and find `testCountSales()`.

```swift
func testCountSales() {
  measureMetrics([.wallClockTime],
                 automaticallyStartMeasuring: false) {

    let employee = getEmployee()
    let employeeDetails = EmployeeDetailViewController()
    startMeasuring()
    _ = employeeDetails.salesCountForEmployee(employee)
    stopMeasuring()
  }
}
```

Like the previous example, this function is using `measureMetrics` to see how long a single function takes to run. The test gets an employee from a convenience method, creates an `EmployeeDetailViewController`, begins measuring and then calls the method in question.

From Xcode's menu bar, select **Product** and then **Test**, or press ⌘ + U. This will build the app and run the test.

Once the test has finished running, you'll see a time next to this test method, as before.

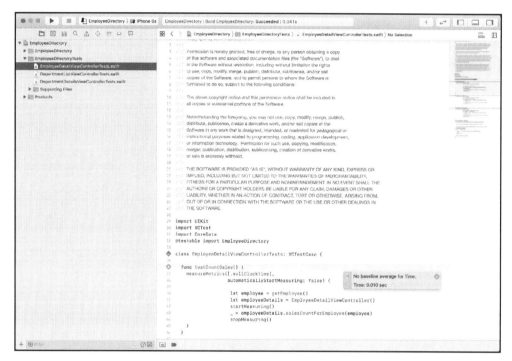

The performance is not too bad — but there is still some room for improvement.

Changes to improve performance

In the previous example, you used NSExpression to group the data and provide a count of employees by department instead of returning the actual records themselves. You'll do the same thing here.

Open **EmployeeDetailViewController.swift** and add the following code to the class below the `salesCountForEmployee(_:)` method.

```
func salesCountForEmployeeFast(_ employee: Employee) -> String {
```

```
let fetchRequest: NSFetchRequest<Sale> = Sale.fetchRequest()
fetchRequest.predicate = NSPredicate(
  format: "%K = %@",
  argumentArray: [#keyPath(Sale.employee), employee])

let context = employee.managedObjectContext!

do {
  let results = try context.count(for: fetchRequest)
  return "\(results)"
} catch let error as NSError {
  print("Error: \(error.localizedDescription)")
  return "0"
}
}
```

This code is very similar to the function you reviewed in the last section. The primary difference is that instead of calling execute(_:), you now call count(for:). Find the following line of code in configureView():

```
salesCountLabel.text = salesCountForEmployee(employee)
```

This line of code uses the old sales count function to populate the label on the department details screen. Replace it by calling the function you just created:

```
salesCountLabel.text = salesCountForEmployeeFast(employee)
```

Verify the changes

Now that you've made the necessary changes to the project, it's once again time to see if you've improved the app. Open **EmployeeDetailViewControllerTests.swift** and add a new function to test the salesCountForEmployeeFast function you just created.

```
func testCountSalesFast() {
  measureMetrics([.wallClockTime],
             automaticallyStartMeasuring: false) {

    let employee = getEmployee()
    let employeeDetails = EmployeeDetailViewController()
    startMeasuring()
    _ = employeeDetails.salesCountForEmployeeFast(employee)
    stopMeasuring()
  }
}
```

This test is identical to the previous one, except it uses the new and, with any luck, faster function.

From Xcode's menu bar, select **Product** and then **Test**, or press ⌘U. This will build the app and run the test.

Looks great — another performance improvement under your belt!

Using relationships

The code above is fast, but the faster method still seems like a lot of work. You have to create a fetch request, create a predicate, get a reference to the context, execute the fetch request and get the results out.

The Employee entity has a `sales` property, which holds a `Set` containing objects of type `Sale`. Open **EmployeeDetailViewController.swift** and add the following new method below the `salesCountForEmployeeFast(_:)` method:

```swift
func salesCountForEmployeeSimple(_ employee: Employee)
                                 -> String {
  return "\(employee.sales!.count)"
}
```

That looks better. By using the sales relationship on the Employee entity, the code is much simpler — and easier to comprehend.

Update the view controller and tests to use this method instead, following the same pattern as above.

Check out the change in performance now.

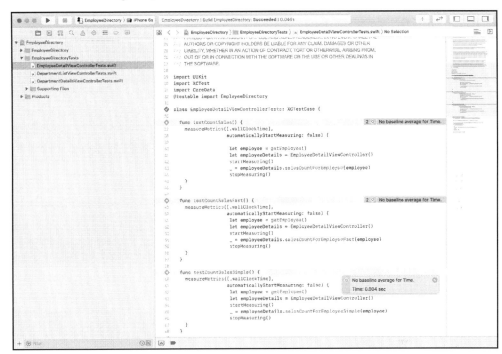

Key points

- Most implementations of Core Data are fast and light already, due to Core Data's built-in optimizations, such as faulting.

- When making improvements to Core Data performance you should measure, make targeted changes and then measure again to validate your changes had the intended impact.

- Small changes to the data model, such as moving large binary blobs to other entities, can improve performance.

- For optimal performance, you should limit the amount of data you fetch to the minimum needed: the more data you fetch, the longer the fetch will take.

- Performance is a balance between memory and speed. When using Core Data in your apps, always keep this balance in mind.

Challenge

Using the techniques you just learned, try to improve the performance of the
`DepartmentDetailsViewController` class. Don't forget to write tests to measure
the before and after execution times. As a hint, there are many methods that provide
counts, rather than the full records; these can probably be optimized somehow to
avoid loading the contents of the records.

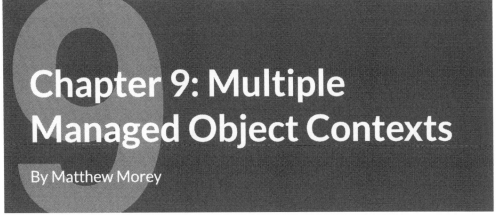

Chapter 9: Multiple Managed Object Contexts

By Matthew Morey

A managed object context is an in-memory scratchpad for working with your managed objects. In Chapter 3, "The Core Data Stack", you learned how the managed object context fits in with the other classes in the Core Data stack.

Most apps need just a single managed object context. The default configuration in most Core Data apps is a single managed object context associated with the main queue. Multiple managed object contexts make your apps harder to debug; it's not something you'd use in every app, in every situation.

That being said, certain situations do warrant the use of more than one managed object context. For example, long-running tasks, such as exporting data, will block the main thread of apps that use only a single main-queue managed object context and cause the UI to stutter.

In other situations, such as when edits are being made to user data, it's helpful to treat a managed object context as a set of changes that the app can discard if it no longer needs them. Using child contexts makes this possible.

In this chapter, you'll learn about multiple managed object contexts by taking a journaling app for surfers and improving it in several ways by adding multiple contexts.

Note: If common Core Data phrases such as managed object subclass and persistent store coordinator don't ring any bells, or if you're unsure what a Core Data stack is supposed to do, you may want to read or reread the first three chapters of this book before proceeding. This chapter covers advanced topics and assumes you already know the basics.

Getting started

This chapter's starter project is a simple journal app for surfers. After each surf session, a surfer can use the app to create a new journal entry that records marine parameters, such as swell height or period, and rate the session from 1 to 5. Dude, if you're not fond of hanging ten and getting barreled, no worries, brah. Just replace the surfing terminology with your favorite hobby of choice!

Introducing SurfJournal

Go to this chapter's files and find the **SurfJournal** starter project. Open the project, then build and run the app.

On startup, the application lists all previous surf session journal entries. Tapping a row brings up the detail view of a surf session with the ability to make edits.

As you can see, the sample app works and has data. Tapping the Export button on the top-left exports the data to a comma-separated values (CSV) file. Tapping the plus (+) button on the top-right adds a new journal entry. Tapping a row in the list opens the entry in edit mode, where you can change or view the details of a surf session.

Although the sample project appears simple, it actually does a lot and will serve as a good base to add multi-context support. First, let's make sure you have a good understanding of the various classes in the project.

Open the project navigator and take a look at the full list of files in the starter project:

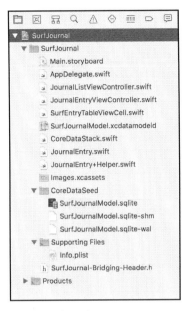

Before jumping into the code, take a brief moment to go over what each class does for you out of the box. If you've completed the earlier chapters, you should find most of these classes familiar:

- **AppDelegate**: On first launch, the app delegate creates the Core Data stack and sets the `coreDataStack` property on the primary view controller `JournalListViewController`.

- **CoreDataStack**: As in previous chapters, this object contains the cadre of Core Data objects known as the **stack**. Unlike in previous chapters, this time the stack installs a database that already has data in it on first launch. No need to worry about this just yet; you'll see how it works shortly.

- **JournalListViewController**: The sample project is a one-page, table-based application. This file represents that table. If you're curious about its UI elements, head over to **Main.storyboard**. There's a table view controller embedded in a navigation controller and a single prototype cell of type **SurfEntryTableViewCell**.

- **JournalEntryViewController**: This class handles creating and editing surf journal entries. You can see its UI in **Main.storyboard**.

- **JournalEntry**: This class represents a surf journal entry. It's an `NSManagedObject` subclass with six properties for attributes: `date`, `height`, `location`, `period`, `rating` and `wind`. If you're curious about this class's entity definition, check out **SurfJournalModel.xcdatamodel**.

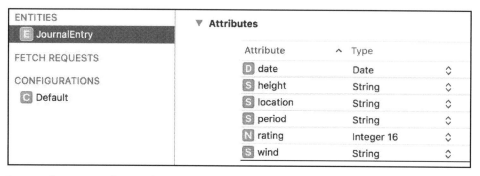

- **JournalEntry+Helper**: This is an extension to the `JournalEntry` object. It includes the CSV export method `csv()` and the `stringForDate()` helper method. These methods are implemented in the extension to avoid being destroyed when you make changes to the Core Data model.

There was already a significant amount of data when you first launched the app.

While the projects in some of the previous chapters import seed data from a JSON file, this sample project comes with a seeded Core Data database.

The Core Data stack

Open **CoreDataStack.swift** and find the following code in `seedCoreDataContainerIfFirstLaunch()`:

```
// 1
let previouslyLaunched =
  UserDefaults.standard.bool(forKey: "previouslyLaunched")
if !previouslyLaunched {
  UserDefaults.standard.set(true, forKey: "previouslyLaunched")

  // Default directory where the CoreDataStack will store its
files
  let directory = NSPersistentContainer.defaultDirectoryURL()
  let url = directory.appendingPathComponent(
    modelName + ".sqlite")

  // 2: Copying the SQLite file
```

```
let seededDatabaseURL = Bundle.main.url(
  forResource: modelName,
  withExtension: "sqlite")!

_ = try? FileManager.default.removeItem(at: url)

do {
  try FileManager.default.copyItem(at: seededDatabaseURL,
                                   to: url)
} catch let nserror as NSError {
  fatalError("Error: \(nserror.localizedDescription)")
}
```

As you can see, this chapter's version of **CoreDataStack.swift** is a little different:

1. You first check UserDefaults for the previouslyLaunched boolean value. If the current execution is indeed the app's first launch, the Bool will be false, making the if statement true. On first launch, the first thing you do is set previouslyLaunched to true so the seeding operation never happens again.

2. You then copy the SQLite seed file **SurfJournalModel.sqlite**, included with the app bundle, to the directory returned by the Core Data-provided method NSPersistentContainer.defaultDirectoryURL().

Now view the rest of seedCoreDataContainerIfFirstLaunch():

```
// 3: Copying the SHM file
let seededSHMURL = Bundle.main.url(forResource: modelName,
  withExtension: "sqlite-shm")!
let shmURL = directory.appendingPathComponent(
  modelName + ".sqlite-shm")

_ = try? FileManager.default.removeItem(at: shmURL)

do {
  try FileManager.default.copyItem(at: seededSHMURL,
                                   to: shmURL)
} catch let nserror as NSError {
  fatalError("Error: \(nserror.localizedDescription)")
}

// 4: Copying the WAL file
let seededWALURL = Bundle.main.url(forResource: modelName,
  withExtension: "sqlite-wal")!
let walURL = directory.appendingPathComponent(
  modelName + ".sqlite-wal")

_ = try? FileManager.default.removeItem(at: walURL)

do {
```

```
        try FileManager.default.copyItem(at: seededWALURL,
                                          to: walURL)
    } catch let nserror as NSError {
        fatalError("Error: \(nserror.localizedDescription)")
    }

    print("Seeded Core Data")
}
```

3. Once the copy of **SurfJournalModel.sqlite** has succeeded, you then copy over the support file **SurfJournalModel.sqlite-shm**.

4. Finally, you copy over the remaining support file **SurfJournalModel.sqlite-wal**.

The only reason **SurfJournalModel.sqlite**, **SurfJournalModel.sqlite-shm** or **SurfJournalModel.sqlite-wal** would fail to copy on first launch is if something really bad happened, such as disk corruption from cosmic radiation. In that case, the device, including any apps, would likely also fail. If the files fail to copy, there's no point in continuing, so the catch blocks call fatalError.

> **Note:** Developers often frown upon using abort and fatalError, as it confuses users by causing the app to quit suddenly and without explanation. This is one scenario where fatalError is acceptable, since the app needs Core Data to work. If an app requires Core Data and Core Data isn't working, there's no point in letting the app continue on, only to fail sometime later in a non-deterministic way.
>
> Calling fatalError, at the very least, generates a stack trace, which can be helpful when trying to fix the problem. If your app has support for remote logging or crash reporting, you should log any relevant information that might be helpful for debugging before calling fatalError.

To support concurrent reads and writes, the persistent SQLite store in this sample app uses SHM (shared memory file) and WAL (write-ahead logging) files. You don't need to know how these extra files work, but you *do* need to be aware of their existence, and that you need to copy them over when seeding the database. If you fail to copy over these files, the app will work, but it might be missing data.

Now that you know something about beginning with a seeded database, you'll learn about multiple managed object contexts by working on a temporary private context.

Doing work in the background

If you haven't done so already, tap the **Export** button at the top-left and then immediately try to scroll the list of surf session journal entries. Notice anything? The export operation takes several seconds, and it prevents the UI from responding to touch events such as scrolling.

The UI is blocked during the export operation because both the export operation and UI are using the main queue to perform their work. This is the default behavior.

The traditional way to fix this is to use Grand Central Dispatch to run the export operation on a background queue. However, Core Data managed object contexts are not thread-safe. That means you can't just dispatch to a background queue and use the same Core Data stack.

The solution is simple: use a private background queue rather than the main queue for the export operation. This will keep the main queue free for the UI to use. But before you jump in and fix the problem, you need to understand how the export operation works.

Exporting data

Start by viewing how the app creates the CSV strings for the `JournalEntry` entity. Open **JournalEntry+Helper.swift** and find `csv()`:

```swift
func csv() -> String {
  let coalescedHeight = height ?? ""
  let coalescedPeriod = period ?? ""
  let coalescedWind = wind ?? ""
  let coalescedLocation = location ?? ""
  let coalescedRating: String
  if let rating = rating?.int16Value {
    coalescedRating = String(rating)
  } else {
    coalescedRating = ""
  }

  return "\(stringForDate()),\(coalescedHeight),\
(coalescedPeriod),\(coalescedWind),\(coalescedLocation),\
(coalescedRating)\n"
}
```

As you can see, `JournalEntry` returns a comma-separated string of the entity's attributes. Because the `JournalEntry` attributes are allowed to be `nil`, the function uses the nil coalescing operator (`??`) to export an empty string instead of an unhelpful debug message that the attribute is `nil`.

> **Note**: The nil coalescing operator (`??`) unwraps an optional if it contains a value; otherwise it returns a default value. For example, the following: `let coalescedHeight = height != nil ? height! : ""` can be shortened using the nil coalescing operator to: `let coalescedHeight = height ?? ""`.

That's how the app creates the CSV strings for an individual journal entry, but how does the app save the CSV file to disk? Open **JournalListViewController.swift** and find the following code in `exportCSVFile()`:

```
// 1
let context = coreDataStack.mainContext
var results: [JournalEntry] = []
do {
  results = try context.fetch(self.surfJournalFetchRequest())
} catch let error as NSError {
  print("ERROR: \(error.localizedDescription)")
}

// 2
let exportFilePath = NSTemporaryDirectory() + "export.csv"
let exportFileURL = URL(fileURLWithPath: exportFilePath)
FileManager.default.createFile(atPath: exportFilePath,
  contents: Data(), attributes: nil)
```

Going through the CSV export code step-by-step:

1. First, retrieve all `JournalEntry` entities by executing a fetch request.

   The fetch request is the same one used by the fetched results controller. Therefore, you reuse the `surfJournalFetchRequest` method to create the request to avoid duplication.

2. Next, create the URL for the exported CSV file by appending the file name ("export.csv") to the output of the `NSTemporaryDirectory` method.

   The path returned by `NSTemporaryDirectory` is a unique directory for temporary file storage. This a good place for files that can easily be generated again and don't need to be backed up by iTunes or to iCloud.

After creating the export URL, call `createFile(atPath:contents:attributes:)` to create the empty file where you'll store the exported data. If a file already exists at the specified file path, this method will remove it first.

Once the app has the empty file, it can write the CSV data to disk:

```
// 3
let fileHandle: FileHandle?
do {
  fileHandle = try FileHandle(forWritingTo: exportFileURL)
} catch let error as NSError {
  print("ERROR: \(error.localizedDescription)")
  fileHandle = nil
}

if let fileHandle = fileHandle {
  // 4
  for journalEntry in results {
    fileHandle.seekToEndOfFile()
    guard let csvData = journalEntry
      .csv()
      .data(using: .utf8, allowLossyConversion: false) else {
        continue
    }

    fileHandle.write(csvData)
  }

  // 5
  fileHandle.closeFile()

  print("Export Path: \(exportFilePath)")
  self.navigationItem.leftBarButtonItem =
    self.exportBarButtonItem()
  self.showExportFinishedAlertView(exportFilePath)

} else {
  self.navigationItem.leftBarButtonItem =
    self.exportBarButtonItem()
}
```

Here's how the file-handling works:

3. First, the app needs to create a file handler for writing, which is simply an object that handles the low-level disk operations necessary for writing data. To create a file handler for writing, use the `FileHandle(forWritingTo:)` initializer.

4. Next, iterate over all `JournalEntry` entities.

   During each iteration, you attempt to create a UTF8-encoded string using `csv()` on `JournalEntry` and `data(using:allowLossyConversion:)` on `String`.

   If it's successful, you write the UTF8 string to disk using the file handler `write()` method.

5. Finally, close the export file-writing file handler, since it's no longer needed.

Once the app has written all the data to disk, it shows an alert dialog with the exported file path.

Note: This alert controller with the export path is fine for learning purposes, but for a real app, you'll need to provide the user with a way to retrieve the exported CSV file, for example using `UIActivityViewController`.

To open the exported CSV file, use Excel, Numbers or your favorite text editor to navigate to and open the file specified in the alert dialog. If you open the file in Numbers you will see the following:

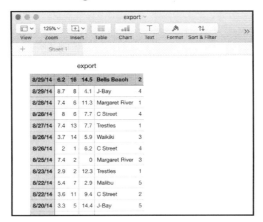

Now that you've seen how the app currently exports data, it's time to make some improvements.

Exporting in the background

You want the UI to continue working while the export is happening. To fix the UI problem, you'll perform the export operation on a private background context instead of on the main context.

Open **JournalListViewController.swift** and find the following code in `exportCSVFile()`:

```
// 1
let context = coreDataStack.mainContext
var results: [JournalEntry] = []
do {
  results = try context.fetch(self.surfJournalFetchRequest())
} catch let error as NSError {
  print("ERROR: \(error.localizedDescription)")
}
```

As you saw earlier, this code retrieves all of the journal entries by calling `fetch()` on the managed object context.

Next, replace the above code with the following:

```
// 1
coreDataStack.storeContainer.performBackgroundTask { context in
```

```
var results: [JournalEntry] = []
do {
  results = try context.fetch(self.surfJournalFetchRequest())
} catch let error as NSError {
  print("ERROR: \(error.localizedDescription)")
}
```

Instead of using the main managed object context also used by the UI, you're now calling `performBackgroundTask(_:)` on the stack's persistent store container. This creates a new managed object context and passes it into the closure.

The context created by `performBackgroundTask(_:)` is on a private queue, which doesn't block the main UI queue. The code in the closure is run on that private queue.

You could also manually create a new temporary private context with a concurrency type of `.privateQueueConcurrencyType` instead of using `performBackgroundTask(_:)`.

> **Note**: There are two concurrency types a managed object context can use:
>
> **Private Queue** specifies the context that will be associated with a private dispatch queue instead of the main queue. This is the type of queue you just used to move the export operation off of the main queue so it would no longer interfere with the UI.
>
> **Main Queue**, the default type, specifies that the context will be associated with the main queue. This type is what the main context (`coreDataStack.mainContext`) uses. Any UI operation, such as creating the fetched results controller for the table view, must use a context of this type.
>
> Contexts and their managed objects must **only** be accessed from the correct queue. `NSManagedObjectContext` has `perform(_:)` and `performAndWait(_:)` to direct work to the correct queue. You can add the launch argument `-com.apple.CoreData.ConcurrencyDebug 1` to your app's scheme to catch mistakes in the debugger.

Next, find the following code in the same method:

```
print("Export Path: \(exportFilePath)")
self.navigationItem.leftBarButtonItem =
  self.exportBarButtonItem()
self.showExportFinishedAlertView(exportFilePath)
} else {
self.navigationItem.leftBarButtonItem =
  self.exportBarButtonItem()
}
```

Replace the code with the following:

```
print("Export Path: \(exportFilePath)")
// 6
DispatchQueue.main.async {
  self.navigationItem.leftBarButtonItem =
    self.exportBarButtonItem()
  self.showExportFinishedAlertView(exportFilePath)
}
} else {
DispatchQueue.main.async {
  self.navigationItem.leftBarButtonItem =
    self.exportBarButtonItem()
}
}
} // 7 Closing brace for performBackgroundTask
```

To finish off the task:

6. You should always perform all operations related to the UI on the main queue, such as showing an alert view when the export operation is finished; otherwise, unpredictable things might happen. Use `DispatchQueue.main.async` to show the final alert view message on the main queue.

7. Finally, add a closing curly brace to close the block you opened earlier in step 1 via the `performBackgroundTask(_:)` call.

Now that you've moved the export operation to a new context with a private queue, build and run to see if it works!

You should see exactly what you saw before:

Tap the Export button in the top left, and immediately try to scroll the list of surf session journal entries. Notice anything different this time? The export operation still takes several seconds to complete, but the table view continues to scroll during this time. The export operation is no longer blocking the UI.

Cowabunga, dude! Gnarly job making the UI more responsive.

You've just witnessed how doing work on a private background queue can improve a user's experience with your app. Now you'll expand on the use of multiple contexts by examining a child context.

Editing on a scratchpad

Right now, SurfJournal uses the main context (`coreDataStack.mainContext`) when creating a new journal entry or viewing an existing one. There's nothing wrong with this approach; the starter project works as-is.

For journaling-style apps like this one, you can simplify the app architecture by thinking of edits or new entries as a set of changes, like a scratch pad. As the user edits the journal entry, you update the attributes of the managed object.

Once the changes are complete, you either save them or throw them away, depending on what the user wants to do.

You can think of child managed object contexts as temporary scratch pads that you can either discard completely, or save and send the changes to the parent context.

But what *is* a child context, technically?

All managed object contexts have a parent store from which you can retrieve and change data in the form of managed objects, such as the `JournalEntry` objects in this project. Typically, the parent store is a persistent store coordinator, which is the case for the main context provided by the `CoreDataStack` class. Alternatively, you can set the parent store for a given context to another managed object context, making it a child context.

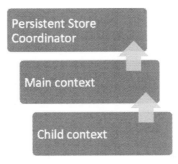

When you save a child context, the changes only go to the parent context. Changes to the parent context won't be sent to the persistent store coordinator until the parent context is saved.

Before you jump in and add a child context, you need to understand how the current viewing and editing operation works.

Viewing and editing

The first part of the operation requires segueing from the main list view to the journal detail view.

Open **JournalListViewController.swift** and find `prepare(for:sender:)`:

```
// 1
if segue.identifier == "SegueListToDetail" {
  // 2
  guard let navigationController =
    segue.destination as? UINavigationController,
    let detailViewController =
```

```
        navigationController.topViewController
          as? JournalEntryViewController,
      let indexPath = tableView.indexPathForSelectedRow else {
        fatalError("Application storyboard mis-configuration")
      }
      // 3
      let surfJournalEntry =
        fetchedResultsController.object(at: indexPath)
      // 4
      detailViewController.journalEntry = surfJournalEntry
      detailViewController.context =
        surfJournalEntry.managedObjectContext
      detailViewController.delegate = self
```

Taking the segue code step-by-step:

1. There are two segues: **SegueListToDetail** and **SegueListToDetailAdd**. The first, shown in the previous code block, runs when the user taps on a row in the table view to view or edit a previous journal entry.

2. Next, you get a reference to the JournalEntryViewController the user is going to end up seeing. It's presented inside a navigation controller so there's some unpacking to do. This code also verifies that there's a selected index path in the table view.

3. Next, you get the JournalEntry selected by the user, using the fetched results controller's object(at:) method.

4. Finally, you set all required variables on the JournalEntryViewController instance. The surfJournalEntry variable corresponds to the JournalEntry entity resolved in step 3. The context variable is the managed object context to be used for any operation; for now, it just uses the main context. The JournalListViewController sets itself as the delegate of the JournalEntryViewController so it can be informed when the user has completed the edit operation.

SegueListToDetailAdd is similar to **SegueListToDetail**, except the app creates a new JournalEntry entity instead of retrieving an existing one.

The app executes **SegueListToDetailAdd** when the user taps the plus (+) button on the top-right to create a new journal entry.

Now that you know how both segues work, open **JournalEntryViewController.swift** and look at the JournalEntryDelegate protocol at the top of the file:

```
protocol JournalEntryDelegate {
  func didFinish(viewController: JournalEntryViewController,
```

```
                         didSave: Bool)
  }
```

The `JournalEntryDelegate` protocol is very short and consists of only one method: `didFinish(viewController:didSave:)`. This method, which the protocol requires the delegate to implement, indicates if the user is done editing or viewing a journal entry and whether any changes should be saved.

To understand how `didFinish(viewController:didSave:)` works, switch back to **JournalListViewController.swift** and find that method:

```swift
func didFinish(viewController: JournalEntryViewController,
               didSave: Bool) {
  // 1
  guard didSave,
    let context = viewController.context,
    context.hasChanges else {
      dismiss(animated: true)
      return
  }
  // 2
  context.perform {
    do {
      try context.save()
    } catch let error as NSError {
      fatalError("Error: \(error.localizedDescription)")
    }
    // 3
    self.coreDataStack.saveContext()
  }
  // 4
  dismiss(animated: true)
}
```

Taking each numbered comment in turn:

1. First, use a `guard` statement to check the `didSave` parameter. This will be `true` if the user taps the Save button instead of the Cancel button, so the app should save the user's data. The guard statement also uses the `hasChanges` property to check if anything's changed; if nothing has changed, there's no need to waste time doing more work.

2. Next, save the `JournalEntryViewController` context inside of a `perform(_:)` closure. The code sets this context to the main context; in this case it's a bit redundant since there's only one context, but this doesn't change the behavior.

Once you add a child context to the workflow later on, the
`JournalEntryViewController` context will be different from the main context,
making this code necessary.

```
If the save fails, call `fatalError` to abort the app with the
relevant error information.
```

3. Next, save the main context via `saveContext`, defined in **CoreDataStack.swift**,
    persisting any edits to disk.

4. Finally, dismiss the `JournalEntryViewController`.

> **Note**: If a managed object context is of type `MainQueueConcurrencyType`, you
> don't *have* to wrap code in `perform(_:)`, but it doesn't hurt to use it.
>
> If you don't know what type the context will be, as is the case in
> `didFinish(viewController:didSave:)`, it's safest to use `perform(_:)` so it
> will work with both parent and child contexts.

There's a problem with the above implementation — have you spotted it?

When the app adds a new journal entry, it creates a new object and adds it to the
managed object context. If the user taps the Cancel button, the app won't save the
context, but the new object will still be present. If the user then adds and saves
another entry, the canceled object will *still* be present! You won't see it in the UI
unless you've got the patience to scroll all the way to the end, but it will show up at
the bottom of the CSV export.

You could solve this problem by deleting the object when the user cancels the view
controller. But what if the changes were complex, involved multiple objects, or
required you to alter properties of an object as part of the editing workflow? Using a
child context will help you manage these complex situations with ease.

Using child contexts for sets of edits

Now that you know how the app currently edits and creates `JournalEntry` entities,
you'll modify the implementation to use a child managed object context as a
temporary scratch pad.

It's easy to do — you simply need to modify the segues. Open
JournalListViewController.swift and find the following code for
SegueListToDetail in `prepare(for:sender:)`:

```
detailViewController.journalEntry = surfJournalEntry
detailViewController.context =
  surfJournalEntry.managedObjectContext
detailViewController.delegate = self
```

Next, replace that code with the following:

```
// 1
let childContext = NSManagedObjectContext(
  concurrencyType: .mainQueueConcurrencyType)
childContext.parent = coreDataStack.mainContext

// 2
let childEntry = childContext.object(
  with: surfJournalEntry.objectID) as? JournalEntry

// 3
detailViewController.journalEntry = childEntry
detailViewController.context = childContext
detailViewController.delegate = self
```

Here's the play-by-play:

1. First, you create a new managed object context named `childContext` with a `.mainQueueConcurrencyType`. Here you set a parent context instead of a persistent store coordinator as you would normally do when creating a managed object context. Here, you set `parent` to `mainContext` of your `CoreDataStack`.

2. Next, you retrieve the relevant journal entry using the child context's `object(with:)` method. You must use `object(with:)` to retrieve the journal entry because managed objects are specific to the context that created them. However, `objectID` values are not specific to a single context, so you can use them when you need to access objects in multiple contexts.

3. Finally, you set all required variables on the `JournalEntryViewController` instance. This time, you use `childEntry` and `childContext` instead of the original `surfJournalEntry` and `surfJournalEntry.managedObjectContext`.

> **Note**: You might be wondering why you need to pass *both* the managed object and the managed object context to the `detailViewController`, since managed objects already have a context variable. This is because managed objects only have a weak reference to the context. If you don't pass the context, ARC will remove the context from memory (since nothing else is retaining it) and the app will not behave as you expect.

Build and run your app; it should work exactly as before. In this case, no visible changes to the app are a good thing; the user can still tap on a row to view and edit a surf session journal entry.

By using a child context as a container for the journal edits, you've reduced the complexity of your app's architecture. With the edits on a separate context, canceling or saving managed object changes is trivial.

Nice work, dude! You're no longer a kook when it comes to multiple managed object contexts. Bodacious!

Key points

- A managed object context is an in-memory scratchpad for working with your managed objects.

- Private background contexts can be used to prevent blocking the main UI.

- Contexts are associated with specific queues and should only be accessed on those queues.

- Child contexts can simplify an app's architecture by making saving or throwing away edits easy.

- Managed objects are tightly bound to their context, and can't be used with other contexts.

- Surfers talk funny.

Challenge

With your newfound knowledge, try to update **SegueListToDetailAdd** to use a child context when adding a new journal entry.

Just like before, you'll need to create a child context that has the main context as its parent. You'll also need to remember to create the new entry on the correct context.

If you get stuck, check out the project with the challenge solution in the folder for this chapter — but give it your best shot first!

Conclusion

We hope this book has helped you get up to speed with Core Data and Swift! You're well on your way to developing your own high-performance apps with well-designed models and unit tests.

As you've seen, you can use Core Data to model all kinds of data — from names and addresses to images and the relationships in between. We encourage you to find where Core Data and its object graph-based persistence can work for you and give it a try.

If you have any questions or comments as you continue to use Core Data, please stop by our forums at http://forums.raywenderlich.com.

Thank you again for purchasing this book. Your continued support is what makes the tutorials, books, videos and other things we do at raywenderlich.com possible — we truly appreciate it!

Wishing you speed, stability and smooth migrations in all your Core Data adventures,

– Pietro, Aaron, Matthew, Rich, Darren and Chris

The *Core Data by Tutorials* team

Printed in Poland
by Amazon Fulfillment
Poland Sp. z o.o., Wrocław